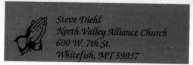

PROPHECY

Things

To

Come

PROPHECY

Things To Come

- A STUDY GUIDE -

By James L. Boyer

Professor of Greek and New Testament

Grace Theological Seminary

Winona Lake, Indiana

Published by

   Books

Winona Lake, Indiana 46590

TO THE

NATIONAL FELLOWSHIP OF BRETHREN CHURCHES

whose unashamed stand on the

Holy Scriptures,

"The Bible, the whole Bible, and nothing but the Bible"

is so deeply appreciated,

I gratefully dedicate this book.

ISBN: 0-88469-006-7

First Printing, October 1973
Second Printing, February 1974

Copyright 1973
BMH Books
Winona Lake, Indiana
Printed in U.S.A.

Foreword

To know the future—is a subject that holds great fascination to the general public. Throughout the ages of man there have been those who promised to be able to foretell. Most have been doomed to failure; a select group, the true prophets of God, have been the exception.

The predictions found in the Word of God are in a class by themselves. It is in God's Word where truths are unfolded and prophecies are made that never fail. This study guide by Dr. James Boyer deals with some of the major themes of Bible prophecy, and we know it will hold for you hours of profitable Bible study.

It may be used as a self-study guide for an individual, thus daily Bible readings have been incorporated with each lesson. It may be used for group study in leading small study classes through the major topics of Bible prophecy. You will also note it is divided into thirteen chapters making it appropriate for a Sunday School class to use in a quarter of study.

Whichever way you may desire to use the book, the end result will be the same. You will know more about God and His work with mankind—both today and in the future.

Charles W. Turner
Editor
BMH Books

Table of Contents

1

Predictive Prophecy:
Its Nature and Importance

SUGGESTED BACKGROUND DEVOTIONAL READING

Monday—Fortune-telling Forbidden (Deut. 18:9-14)
Tuesday—Ministry of the Prophet (Deut. 18:15-22)
Wednesday—Fulfilled Prophecy (Ezek. 26:1-14)
Thursday—A More Sure Word (II Peter 1:16-21)
Friday—Searching Their Writings (I Peter 1:10-16)
Saturday—Words of the Holy Prophets (II Peter 3:1-10)
Sunday—Therefore Be Diligent (II Peter 3:11-18)

INTRODUCTION

This series of studies will deal with a subject of great interest. Most people are concerned about what the future holds and would like to know what is going to happen. But these studies are not merely to satisfy curiosity. They deal with matters of great importance, and they involve very personal and practical values.

THE AIM

In order to have a proper background for the whole series, we need to see that prediction of the future is a part of the whole message which God gave by inspiration to the prophets who spoke forth His Word. This study should increase our appreciation of the Bible as God's Word as we see how Bible predictions have already been exactly fulfilled. In view of man's obvious inability to foretell future events, the Bible's accuracy in doing so is proof that it is God's Word, not man's.

THE DEVELOPMENT

First, our study turns to a passage of Scripture which shows that the ability to correctly prophesy future events is a mark of a true spokesman for God.

Second, we select just one example, from the dozens of such in the Bible, of a predictive prophecy, and show how later history verifies its exact fulfillment.

Third, we turn in the New Testament to see how one of the Lord's apostles evaluated the importance of the prophetic Scriptures.

THE EXPOSITION

I. Only God Can Reveal the Future (Deut. 18)

There will not be time to deal with all of this passage or to look at all the interesting details. Three chief ideas should be made clear.

1. **Israel was forbidden to use fortune-telling to learn the future or any other unknown secrets** (vv. 9-14). Deuteronomy gives us the farewell message of Moses to the children of Israel on the eve of their entrance into the Promised Land. He had led them out of Egypt and for forty years through the terrible experience of the wilderness wanderings. Now God had brought them to the east bank of the Jordan and was ready to take them across into Canaan. But that venture was to be led by another man, Joshua, and Moses gathered the people together to take his farewell and to give them his final words of advice as they entered into the land.

Among the admonitions was this warning against following the abominable practices of the heathen inhabitants of the land. All the practices referred to are forms of fortune-telling, seeking to discover the future or the most favorable course of action by superstitious means. These practices included examining the livers of sacrificial animals, watching the flight of birds, reading the stars, consulting with the spirits of the dead, and contacting demons. Moses warned Israel that all such practices were absolutely forbidden by God; they are abominable to Him.

God still hates every form of fortune-telling. Although the methods have changed slightly, basically, all forms of fortune-telling in use today are merely slight adaptations of the ones described here. Reading palms, tea leaves, cards, astrology and horoscopes, spiritualism, communicating with the spirits of dead relatives, Ouija boards, table tapping, and so forth, are practices absolutely forbidden by God. Whether in fun or in seriousness God's people should have nothing to do with them.

2. **Instead of these, God gave Israel a prophet to speak His words and to**

reveal His will (vv. 15, 18). God's people were shut up to one method of learning what the future held and how they should conduct their lives. God himself would tell them all they needed to know. He would do this through His own appointed mouthpiece, His prophet. When Israel wanted to know something, she could come to God's prophet.

In that day, Moses exercised the office of prophet. These verses tell us that God would raise up another like Moses after Moses was gone. This no doubt had its first application to that line of true prophets which God gave to Israel through their long history, including Samuel, Elijah, and Isaiah. But its full meaning was realized when Christ himself came to give men God's final revelation of himself and His will.

God's perfect and final revelation has now been incorporated in a Book, the Bible. To us, the application is clear. If we want to know anything about the future, or other spiritual secrets of life, we may go to this Book. We must be satisfied with the answers given there; we are not to seek further information from fortune-tellers. God has told us in this Bible as much as He wants us to know about such things.

True prophets spoke forth God's message to men. God's Spirit so directed and safeguarded their messages that what they said was exactly what He wanted said. Prophecy produced the inspired Scriptures.

3. **The test of a true prophet was his ability to predict future events** (vv. 21-22). Man is notoriously unable to foretell what the future will bring. With all his scientific equipment he is often wrong even about tomorrow's weather, and political forecasts are still more unreliable. But God sees from the vantage point of eternity. The future is as plain to Him as are the present and the past.

So if a prophet predicts that some event will take place, the test of his message is the future. If his prediction does not come to pass, he is proved false; he was not speaking from God. If it comes to pass as prophesied, it proves that the message was from God. One of the most effective proofs of the genuineness of the Scriptures is the fact of fulfilled prophecies.

II. A Remarkable Example of Fulfilled Prophecy (Ezek. 26:1-14)

Of the many that might be used, we select one sample. Ezekiel prophesied the destruction of one of the great cities of his day, the Phoenician city of Tyre. The prophecy was given in the eleventh year of King Jehoiachin's captivity (v. 1), or about 587 B.C.

As we read the prophecy we are struck with the peculiar change of subject. In verses 3-6 the ones who are to bring about the destruction of Tyre are spoken of in the plural: "Many nations [v. 3] . . . they [v. 4] . . . the nations" (v. 5). Then in verses 7-11 this plural subject is dropped and a singular subject is used: "Nebuchadrezzar [v. 7] . . . he" (vv. 8, 9, 10, 11). In verses 12-14 the prophet returns to the plural subject "they," that is, the "many nations" of verses 3-6. Thus, the prophet indicates by his choice of words that there is a twofold destruction in store for this great city.

When we look at the fulfillment, it all becomes clear. One year after the prophecy was given, Nebuchadnezzar came up through the whole seacoast, capturing everything as he went except Tyre. This city resisted his attack and he besieged it for twelve or thirteen years. Then, when it appeared they could hold out no longer, the king of Tyre moved the government, its treasures, and many of its people out of the city on the mainland to an island fortress one-half mile out in the Mediterranean Sea. When Nebuchadnezzar captured the city he was unable to defeat the king of Tyre or to touch the city's great wealth. The prophet Ezekiel refers to this in 29:17-18.

This, however, left a large part of the prophecy concerning Tyre unfulfilled, and it remained so for over two hundred fifty years. Perhaps some unbeliever might scoff and say that Ezekiel made a shrewd guess as he saw Nebuchadnezzar coming. But no guess can explain the amazing events which began to transpire with the coming of Alexander.

Alexander the Great with an army of thirty to forty thousand men began his triumphal march by invading Asia Minor in 334 B.C. He swept across Asia Minor, through the Cilician Gates into Phoenicia and Syria, encountered the Persian King Darius III at Issus in 333 B.C., and easily defeated over two hundred thousand Persians. To keep control of the sea and to protect his lines of communication, he did not follow the enemy inland but turned and went down the Phoenician coast. Biblus and Sidon surrendered, but Tyre resisted. This angered Alexander, and he began a siege of the city which is described as "the most difficult undertaking in all his wars." Of course, the people of Tyre did again what they had done earlier under Nebuchadnezzar: they moved out to the island fortress. But

Alexander was not to be turned aside. To get to the island he built a causeway through the sea, scraping the ruins and foundations of the mainland city, even the dust of the city, to get materials. The Tyrians with their navy were able once to destroy this bridge, but Alexander got ships from other Phoenician towns that had surrendered and rebuilt the causeway right up to the walls of the island fort. After seven months he succeeded in breaking through.

Ezekiel's prophecy was fulfilled with amazing accuracy. He had said "many nations"; there was Babylon in 572, Persia in 525 and in 351, and then Alexander, with an army made up of many nations, in 333. Ezekiel told of breaking down her walls and towers and scraping her dust into the sea. He spoke of Tyre becoming a spoil to the nations. And although Nebuchadnezzar got no spoil, Alexander did. Six thousand of the city's inhabitants perished by the sword, two thousand were crucified, and thirty thousand women, children, and slaves were sold into captivity.

But even this is not the end. Ezekiel went on to make what is probably the most remarkable prediction of all. Verses 13 and 14 of chapter 26 describe the end of Tyre for all time and make the solemn prediction, ". . . thou shalt be built no more." That makes the prophecy extend down more than two thousand years into our own time. Has it proved true?

According to history Tyre was rebuilt by the Seleucids. In New Testament times it was still a large city (Acts 21:3-4). It was finally destroyed by the Turks in A.D. 1291. Today there is a small Arab seaport, Sours, or Tsur, of five to eight thousand people. But the prophecy has not failed, for these later cities are not located on the ancient site. The causeway built by Alexander has created a sandy isthmus extending out from the mainland and joining the former island to the shore. On this causeway fishermen still spread their nets (Ezek. 26:5). But the ancient city has never been rebuilt, in spite of the fact that a good spring of water is available there.

Tyre's sister city in ancient Phoenicia was Sidon, twenty miles away. Ezekiel also prophesied concerning this city (28:20-23). He spoke of pestilence and blood in the streets, all of which has been abundantly witnessed to by history from then till now. But he said nothing about its not being rebuilt or continuing. And it has continued, is still an important city. How could Ezekiel have known? The answer is obvious: God knew, and He told Ezekiel what to prophesy. "Holy men of God spake as they were moved by the Holy Ghost" (II Peter 1:21).

III. The Importance of the Prophetic Word (II Peter 1:16-21)

This passage from II Peter clearly and vividly calls our attention to the importance of the prophetic Word, the function it is intended to perform, the period of its operation, and the proper manner of handling it.

1. **The relative importance of the prophetic Word** (vv. 16-19). The key to understanding these verses is in verse 19, in the words "a more sure word of prophecy." More sure than what? In verses 16 to 18 Peter tells about his remarkable experience in the Mount of Transfiguration. There he and two of his fellow disciples were eyewitnesses and earwitnesses of Christ's majesty. They saw Jesus transfigured before their eyes, until He shone forth in all the dazzling glory of His essential deity. They remembered He had told them just before (Mark 8:38; 9:1-2) that some of them would not taste of death until they had seen the Son of Man coming in His power and glory. Now they were convinced that this transfigured appearance of Christ was an actual preview of that future coming. So Peter says (v. 16), "We have not followed cunningly devised fables, when we made known unto you the power and coming of our Lord Jesus Christ, but were eyewitnesses of his majesty." Also, they had heard with their ears the supernatural voice from heaven witnessing to the identity of this wonderful person. What could possibly be more sure than such supernaturally attested personal experiences?

Yet, Peter says, we have a "more sure word" than these, the Word of prophecy. That means that the testimony of Scripture, specifically here the prophetic Scripture, is more sure, more authoritative, more convincing than any testimony directly from the life of those who actually experienced miracles and supernatural signs. If Peter and Paul and John and the rest of the apostles all were to appear in person today on a public platform and declare their wonderful experiences, these all would not be as important as the words of this Bible we have had all along! Compare this with what Jesus reported as the words of Abraham to the rich man in Hades (Luke 16:27-31).

In view of this, Peter presses home his exhortation, "whereunto ye do well that ye take heed." Would you listen if God spoke audibly from heaven? Then, even more, listen to what He has said in the Word of prophecy.

2. **The function of the prophetic Word** (v. 19). The sure Word of prophecy is as "a light that shineth in a dark place, until the day dawn, and the day star arise in your hearts." Thus Peter describes its heavenly intended purpose.

This world through which we must pass as pilgrims and sojourners is indeed a dark place. It is dark morally because of sin. Men love darkness rather than light because their deeds are evil. It is dark mentally because of ignorance and superstition. Men cannot read the future, and they often cannot understand the things which are happening to them and around them. It is a dark world spiritually, because it is without God. Men are groping around in this dark night, seeking someone to lead them. You and I, God's people, are the light of the world. We must show them the way to God and to life. We have in our hands the lamp of prophetic truth, shining in a dark place.

It is a lamp only, not a sun that is bright enough to drive away all the darkness. Prophetic Scripture will not light up everything; it will not answer every question that curiosity might raise about the future and its events. But it does give us enough light that we can see to get along through this dark world. It reveals hidden dangers and exposes evil. It allays fears, guards against false hopes, encourages us in the face of trying circumstances. It guides our steps and keeps us from stumbling in the dark. This is really all we need today, for we walk by faith, not by sight.

And it is only temporary, a light shining "until the day dawn." That day will be the second coming of Christ and the fulfillment of all the prophecies related to it. Then the world's night will give way to the new day of the messianic kingdom. The Sun of Righteousness will arise with healing in His rays. When the full light of fulfillment has dawned, there will no longer be needed the precious lamp which has led us while we were in the dark place.

The next phrase has been interpreted many ways. The light of prophecy shines until "the day star arise in your hearts." Perhaps this refers to a secondary purpose of prophecy: not only to point to the second coming of Christ, but also to lead men to receive Christ in their hearts even now. This certainly is a legitimate application. Or, it may refer to the Rapture, the daystar that precedes and heralds the full dawn, which will affect only the believers, the blessed hope which prophecy causes to arise in our hearts.

Thus the purpose of prophetic truth is to light our way and direct our lives through the darkness of this world, pointing us with hope to that blessed day when Jesus will come again. Is it performing its function in our hearts? It will if we let it shine by studying the prophetic Word. So the basic purpose back of this series of studies is intensely practical. This study will help steer you away from mere sensationalism and idle curiosity and emphasize its practical usefulness.

3. **The manner of pursuit of the prophetic Word** (vv. 20-21). Peter closes this section with a warning and a word of instruction as to the proper way to handle prophetic Scripture. It is not "of any private interpretation." This passage has been understood in several ways, more than one of which are possible and express important truths.

Some take it to mean that the prophetic Scriptures are not to be taken alone and interpreted without regard for the rest of Scripture. Always we must safeguard our interpretations of prophecy by comparing them with the full teaching of the whole Bible. God doesn't contradict himself, and if our understanding of any particular prophetic utterance makes it contradict other Bible truth, then our interpretation must be wrong. This, of course, is true, but it should not be pressed to teach that unless a truth is expressed elsewhere in the Bible it is therefore wrong. Some Biblical truths are presented in a single Scripture reference.

Others understand the verse to teach that the prophetic Scriptures are not to be limited to the times or the understanding of the prophet who wrote them. They may have had a personal, direct, private meaning to those to whom they were first uttered; they may have been understood in some particular way at that time. But that does not exhaust their true meaning. Peter spoke of this in his first epistle (I Peter 1:10-12). He pictured the prophets themselves as carefully searching into and studying their own prophecies to try to understand what they meant, and being instructed by the Spirit that they ministered this message not merely to themselves, but also to us many generations later. This, of course, is vigorously denied by the scoffers and unbelievers, but to the believer it is one of the strong proofs of the inspiration of God's Word. If the verse is so understood one must take care that he does not extend this principle to the point that it justifies "spiritualizing" or allegorizing the clear prophetic Scriptures.

Others understand the words "not of any private interpretation" as though they referred to the origin of the prophetic message; it did not come from the prophets themselves, but from the Holy Spirit. That, of course, is true, as the next verse explicitly tells us. But the meaning of the word translated "interpretation" and the present tense of the verb argues strongly that there is more here than simply a repetition of the sense of verse 21.

To the present writer it seems best to understand these words to mean that the prophetic Scripture is not to be understood merely on the human level; it needs the guidance of the Holy Spirit himself, who originally gave it. "The natural man receiveth not the things of the Spirit of God: for they are foolishness unto him: neither can he know them, because they are spiritually discerned" (I Cor. 2:14). Of course, this is true of all spiritual truths, but it is especially true of the prophetic Scriptures. An unsaved man simply doesn't have the capacity to understand prophecy. The study of prophecy is impossible and meaningless to him. The Holy Spirit may use it to arouse his interest and to lead him to Christ, but until he makes that response he cannot be expected to understand. Everyone outside of Christ needs a spiritual awakening and enlightening through faith in Jesus Christ.

The reason given in verse 21 for this warning against "private interpretation" makes it clear that Peter is talking about the necessity of the Spirit's guidance. The prophetic Scriptures did not originate in the first place from man's will. Isaiah did not decide on his own will and initiative that he would write a prediction. Rather, the Holy Spirit prompted him to write; and other "holy men of God spake as they were moved [literally, 'being borne along'] by the Holy Ghost." Man couldn't and didn't write the prophecies by his own will. Neither can he interpret them by his own abilities. He needs the Holy Spirit to guide him into this truth.

Perhaps a warning should be given here against one interpretation of this verse which is certainly false. Some would make this verse say that no individual or private Christian dare try to understand prophecy, that he must rely on "official pronouncements" of a clerical order or of a school of thought. As Protestants we rebel against the notion that a layman is not qualified to use the Scriptures for himself and must depend on "approved explanations" by the authority of the church. But we need also to guard against accepting some theological system, or some prophetic scheme, or some set of notations in a particular version of the Bible, to the point where the Holy Spirit cannot speak to us through His Word. So, don't be afraid to read the Bible, and the prophecies of the Bible, for yourself, and trust the Holy Spirit to guide you into the truth.

SUMMARY

The ability to foretell the future belongs to God alone.

The Bible contains many predictions of the future which have proved absolutely true. Therefore the Bible is of God.

A very large portion of the Bible is prophetic. Evidently God wanted us to know certain facts about the future.

The study of prophecy is not to satisfy our curiosity, but to direct us.

2

Messianic Prophecy:
The First Coming

SUGGESTED BACKGROUND DEVOTIONAL READING

Monday—The Jews Expected Messiah (John 1:19-28)
Tuesday—Are You the Messiah? (Matt. 11:1-6)
Wednesday—Seed of Abraham (Gen. 22:15-18; Gal. 3:16)
Thursday—Seed of David (II Sam. 7:12-16)
Friday—Prophecy of Messiah's Suffering (Isa. 53)
Saturday—Suffering and Glory (Luke 24:25-27, 44-47)
Sunday—Birth Fulfills Prophecy (Matt. 1:18-23)

INTRODUCTION

Jesus Christ is the center of prophecy as He is of the whole Bible. He is the main theme of prophecy; in fact, all prophecy ultimately relates to His person, His work, His history. So our study of prophecy begins with a consideration of His coming as it is foretold in the Scriptures. This subject is usually called messianic prophecy, because the Old Testament Scriptures foretold the coming of one whom God anointed to be His King and the Saviour of mankind. The Hebrew word "Messiah" means "Anointed," or "the Anointed One." Its Greek equivalent is "Christ," which also means the "Anointed One."

THE AIM

Two specific objectives should direct our attention to this study. First, it should serve as a further example of fulfilled prophecy, illustrating and enforcing the inspiration of the Bible and strengthening our conviction that God can and has foretold the future, that the Bible actually does foretell history. Second, this study should point us to Jesus Christ as God's chosen Messiah, sent to be our Saviour.

THE DEVELOPMENT

First, we want to see that when Jesus came into this world nineteen hundred years ago He was *expected.* The people of Israel, even the world in general, had been led to look for the coming of such a one through the prophecies of the Old Testament Scriptures.

Second, we will trace through the earlier parts of the Old Testament a series of prophecies which identify the ancestry and family line of this promised Messiah, serving to identify His Person.

Third, we will see how these predictions flower out into a multitude of details in the later parts of the Old Testament, and begin to divide into two distinct lines of prediction of the coming Messiah, one picturing Him as a glorious king, the other as a humble, suffering servant.

Fourth, we will turn to a couple passages in the New Testament to find the key by which we may be able to distinguish between them and to rightly interpret these prophecies.

And finally, we will look at some of the remarkable details of these prophecies, literally fulfilled at the first advent of Christ.

From the nature of this study it will be necessary to turn to a large number of Scripture passages, rather than to study a few passages in detail.

THE EXPOSITION

I. When Jesus Came, He Was Expected

1. **John 1:19-20, 41, 45; 3:28; 4:25; Matthew 2:4-6.** Without taking time to expound these verses, it is clearly seen that the people in Jesus' day were looking for the coming of some great personage whom they called Messiah. The delegation that visited John the Baptist, Andrew when he went to testify to his brother Simon, Philip in his testimony to Nathanael, the scribes consulted by King Herod, even the Samaritan woman at the well, all were expecting the arrival of this Messiah. Whence did this expectation arise? It could only have been from the prophecies of the Old Testament which foretold His coming.

2. **Matthew 1:22; Mark 1:2; Luke 1:31-33; Acts 2:30-31; Romans 1:2-3.** The Gospel writers and the early preachers of the Gospel clearly claimed that Christ was the fulfillment of the Old Testament predictions of that Messiah. The number of passages here might be multiplied indefi-

nitely; in Matthew's Gospel alone it is specifically claimed at least *sixty* times.

3. **Matthew 11:2-5; Luke 4:16-21; John 5:39, 46.** Jesus himself deliberately applied these Old Testament prophecies to himself and His work. So we have the authority of the Lord Jesus Christ himself when we see in the Old Testament Scriptures predictions of His coming.

II. The Line of Descent of the Messiah Was Predicted

Centuries before the birth of Christ His family and line of descent had been prophesied.

1. **He was to be born of a woman** (Gen. 3:15). This famous prophecy was God's promise that sin's curse would be undone by someone who would be born of a woman: that is, a human being, a member of the human race. All men are born of women (Job 14:1; Matt. 11:11). The expression "seed of the woman," therefore, is probably not to be taken as a direct prophecy of a virgin birth (that is, by woman *alone*), but certainly it is appropriate to such a birth. The fact that the coming redeemer was to be a member of the human race is a significant truth (Heb. 2:16-18).

2. **His family line** (Gen. 12:3; 18:18; 22:16-18; 17:19; 26:4; 28:14; 49:10). Part of the promise God made to Abraham when He called him out of Ur was that "in thy seed shall all the families of the earth be blessed." Thus the promised redeemer was to come through Abraham, for that seed was to be Christ, the Messiah. Of Abraham's descendants God chose Isaac and repeated the promise to him. Of Isaac's twin sons God picked Jacob and again repeated the promise to his seed. Of Jacob's twelve sons God prophetically pointed to the tribe of Judah as the family through whom the line of government was to proceed, until Shiloh would come. This rather mysterious title is variously explained, but it was understood by the Jews as well as the Christians as referring to the Messiah. So the kingly line, the right to rule, and the messianic King are foretold to come from the tribe of Judah.

3. **His throne will be the throne of His father David** (II Sam. 7:12-16). In this important passage we have a most remarkable prophecy. God promised that He himself was going to build the house of David, and establish his throne. He made it clear that this promise was unconditional,

no strings attached. It would be carried through even if David's sons should not follow in the steps of their father. Three times He repeated the solemn assertion that this promise was "for ever." David's house, David's throne, was to stand forever. David would never lack a son to sit upon his throne (Jer. 33:17).

Isaiah, Jeremiah, Ezekiel, and other of the prophets spoke of the Messiah as David's son, a branch or shoot that would come up out of the seemingly dead stump of that fallen house. And after the house of David had gone into eclipse for hundreds of years, when its living representatives were such poor and insignificant people as a carpenter in an obscure village in Nazareth and his espoused bride-to-be, God remembered His promise to David and boldly announced to the Virgin Mary the birth of a wonderful Son, with the words: "He shall be great, and shall be called the Son of the Highest: and the Lord God shall give unto him the throne of his father David: And he shall reign over the house of Jacob for ever; and of his kingdom there shall be no end" (Luke 1:32-33).

Today the genealogies are gone, the house of David forever lost. If Jesus is not the prophesied seed of David, then there never can be such. But David has his Son, and He yet shall reign.

III. Prophecies of the Messiah Multiply

In the later parts of the Old Testament, from the time of David on, there is a great multiplying of prophecies concerning this coming Messiah. Particularly in the Psalms and the prophets are revealed a great mass of minute details regarding the work, the career, and the person of the one who is to come. As we study them, two distinct pictures emerge.

In the majority of these prophecies we are given a picture of a great and glorious, powerful king: great David's greater Son. He is to rule in righteousness and justice and peace forever over the people of Israel and over the whole world. With power He will destroy God's enemies and judge the people. The prophets seem to exhaust human language to describe the glories of that wonderful Golden Age to come, when God's Messiah is on His throne and His kingdom rules over all. For examples of these prophecies turn to Isaiah 9:6-7 and 11:1-9.

But in some of the prophecies this person who was to come is described in the role of a lowly, rejected, suffering servant. He is Jehovah's servant, come to do His will. He is reproached, deserted, and rejected, betrayed by His own familiar friend; cut off, but not for himself; a meek, unresisting lamb led to the slaughter, suffering and dying for the sins of all. The very manner of His death is described with the vividness of an eyewitness. One of the best-known examples of this type of prophecy is Isaiah 53.

With these seemingly contradictory descriptions of the promised Messiah it is little wonder that the Jews were confused. Some of them tried to solve the puzzle by suggesting two Messiahs. Many of them chose to accept those prophecies which spoke of a great king, ignoring the others, fanatically hoping for the coming of an earthly deliverer who would break the yoke of Rome and restore the kingdom of David to Israel. This idea is reflected often in the New Testament. It ultimately so inflamed the passions of the people that open revolt broke out and led to the awful destruction of Jerusalem in A.D. 70. Some Jews repudiated the whole messianic idea and turned to formalism; later this became the official view of organized Judaism.

IV. The Key to Decipher the Puzzle

Actually, the answer to the problem is a simple one, after you learn what it is. And the New Testament very clearly reveals the key. Let us look at a couple key passages.

1. **I Peter 1:10-11.** Peter here pictures the Old Testament prophets as being puzzled by their own prophecies. They studied and searched diligently the prophecies which the Spirit gave them. But please notice the exact nature of their search. It had to do with the *time* element: "Searching what [time], or what manner of time" the Spirit signified when He testified "*beforehand* the sufferings of Christ, and the glory *that should follow.*" Here these two elements of their prophecy are both mentioned, the sufferings and the glory. And the key is the time element: *first* the suffering, *then* the glory.

2. **Luke 24:25-27, 44-47.** This familiar story reveals the same key. These disciples had been looking for the glory of the Messiah and His kingdom. They were not prepared for the suffering. The events of that awful crucifixion day had almost destroyed their hope. Their concept of the Messiah had no place for His shameful death. But Jesus took them

through the prophetic Scriptures of the whole Old Testament, showing them that they ought to believe *all* that the prophets had spoken. The key word in verse 26 is the word "and." "Ought not Christ to have suffered these things, *and* to enter into his glory?" So also in verses 46 and 47. *First* must be the suffering; *then* would come the glory. The key is the *time* element.

3. **Luke 4:16-21**. Again a familiar story shows us the key. At the very outset of Jesus' public ministry He attended His home synagogue at Nazareth and was asked to read the Scripture lesson for the day. He turned to the prophecy of Isaiah, chapter 61, and began to read. But in the middle of the second verse he suddenly stopped reading, closed the book and began to speak: "This day is this scripture fulfilled in your ears." Using the time key now, it becomes clear. The part of the Scripture which He read described the work of the Messiah which Jesus then was beginning to do. But there was another aspect of the Messiah's work which did not belong to that day. So He did not read that. The key to Isaiah's prophecy was the time element. Part of it belonged to one time, the rest of it belonged to another time, and Jesus carefully observed this distinction.

Let us see how this time key unlocks the problem of messianic prophecy. Actually it divides the prophecies into two groups, one group having application to the *first* coming of Christ, when He appeared as a lowly, suffering Saviour; the other group belonging to a later time, when Jesus would come again, this time in power and glory to establish His kingdom. First the suffering, then the glory. All the prophecies are true, all will be fulfilled, all speak of the same Messiah, but not all refer to the same time.

Now that we have the key it is not too difficult to sort out the Old Testament predictions. Pick out the ones which He fulfilled in His first coming; the ones that are left are to be fulfilled at His second coming. And the precise, detailed fulfillment of the former are the best proof of the reliability and literality of the latter. He *did* come; He *will* come again.

V. Prophecies Fulfilled at Christ's First Coming

It will be interesting for you at this point to trace through the passages in the Old Testament which foretell the first advent of the Messiah and check their fulfillment in the New Testament. This may be done with the help of a reference Bible such as Scofield's, or of a subject index or topical index. There are about fifty such passages, some containing many distinct details, so that the number of predictions made about His coming are many times that number. Here we will summarize only a few.

1. **Predictions of His birth**. The most remarkable of these is the prophecy that He should be born of a virgin. The prediction is given in Isaiah 7:14; its fulfillment is recorded in Matthew 1:18, 20, 22-23, and 25. This miraculous sign should convince any fair-minded person of the supernatural nature of this person so born.

The place of His birth was also foretold (Micah 5:2; Matt. 2:4-8). Bethlehem, the ancient home of David, was to be the birthplace of David's greater Son.

Other incidents related to His birth were found to reflect the prophecies of the Old Testament. Isaiah had foreseen the recognition of the promised Messiah by the Gentiles and their kings at His rising (Isa. 60:3), thus anticipating the worship of the Magi and their kingly gifts (Matt. 2:1-2, 11). The flight of Joseph and Mary into Egypt to save the infant Jesus from the plot of Herod recalled the words of the prophet Hosea (11:1). And the massacre of the babies of Bethlehem by Herod was seen as a fulfillment of Jeremiah's words in Jeremiah 31:15.

2. **Predictions of His life and ministry**. The Old Testament writings had closed on an obvious note of expectancy. The last of the prophets had added an interesting detail to the picture of His coming by his announcement that God would send a forerunner to prepare for the Messiah's coming, even stating the identity of that forerunner (Mal. 3:1; 4:5; also Isa. 40:3). The New Testament describes the beginning of Christ's public ministry by introducing a strange person who called himself a "voice crying in the wilderness, prepare ye the way of the Lord." Thus John the Baptist appears as the messenger sent ahead by God to announce the Messiah's coming (Mark 1:1-4; Matt. 11:14). Jesus himself recognized him as such, and announced that this prophecy was to have a more complete fulfillment later when Elijah himself would come to prepare for His second coming.

The prophets had foretold the message and the ministry of the Messiah. When Jesus read the Scripture lesson that Sabbath day in the synagogue in Nazareth at the beginning of His ministry, He turned to a passage in the prophecy of Isaiah (61:1) which told what the Messiah would do when He came—preach the Gospel to the meek, bind up the brokenhearted, and so forth. Then with a simple but dramatic announcement He closed the reading: "This day is this scripture fulfilled in your ears" (Luke 4:16-21). The prophet had painted a glowing picture of the wonderful times of the Messiah when the eyes of the blind would be opened, the deaf would hear, the dumb would be able to speak, and the lame would leap as a hart (Isa. 35:5-6). Hundreds of years later Jesus pointed to these very miracles of healing when He wanted to prove to John that He really was the Messiah they had been looking for (Luke 7:21-22).

3. **Predictions of His suffering and death**. Of all the prophecies fulfilled by Christ at His first coming, those that dealt with His suffering and death were the most numerous and most spectacular. But they were not seen or understood at the time, for the expectations of the Jews were fixed on the more pleasant and desirable picture of the glorious king who would bring justice and peace to their oppressed nation and sit forever on David's throne. Not until after Jesus had actually died and risen again were they able to see that this also was a part of the Old Testament messianic picture.

Isaiah had prophesied that the coming Messiah would be despised and rejected of men, a man of sorrows and acquainted with grief (Isa. 53:3), a stone of stumbling and a rock of offense to many in Israel (Isa. 8:14-15). Before him the Psalmist had spoken of the kings and rulers taking counsel together against the Lord and His Anointed (His Messiah, His Christ; Ps. 2:1-3), of His being a stranger to His brethren and an alien to His mother's children (Ps. 69:8), and had called Him a stone rejected by the builders, although it was the head stone of the corner (Ps. 118:22).

Besides these general references to the humiliation and rejection of the coming Messiah, there were foretold a large number of specific details relating to His death and the accompanying events. I merely list them here, without comment, even though among them are some of the most remarkable fulfillments of prophecy the world has ever seen. (The first reference is the Old Testament prophecy; the New Testament reference tells its fulfillment.)

1. Sold for thirty pieces of silver (Zech. 11:12; Matt. 26:14-15).

2. Betrayed by one of His own friends (Psa. 41:9; 55:12-14; Matt. 26:49-50).

3. Potter's field purchased with the betrayal money (Zech. 11:13; Matt. 27:5-7).

4. Forsaken by all His disciples (Zech. 13:7; Matt. 26:56; Mark 14:27).

5. False witness used against Him (Ps. 35:11; Matt. 26:59-60).

6. Beaten, abused, insulted, spit upon (Isa. 50:6; Matt. 26:67).

7. Wounded and bruised (Isa. 53:5; Matt. 27:26, 29).

8. Silent before His accusers (Isa. 53:7; Matt. 27:12, 14).

9. Weakened by suffering (Ps. 109:24; Luke 23:26).

10. Hands and feet pierced (Ps. 22:16; John 20:25-27).

11. Numbered with transgressors (Isa. 53:12; Mark 15:27-28).

12. Prayed for His persecutors (Isa. 53:12; Luke 23:34).

13. People shook their heads (Ps. 109:25; Matt. 27:39).

14. People mocked and ridiculed Him (Ps. 22:7-8; Matt. 27:41-43).

15. A public spectacle (Ps. 22:17; Luke 23:35).

16. Garments divided by casting lots (Ps. 22:18; John 19:23-24).

17. His cry of anguish (Ps. 22:1; Matt. 27:46).

18. Gall and vinegar given Him (Ps. 69:21; John 19:28-29).

19. He yielded up His spirit to God (Ps. 31:5; Luke 23:46).

20. Friends stood afar off (Ps. 38:11; Luke 23:49).

21. His bones not broken (Ps. 34:20; John 19:33, 36).

22. His side pierced (Zech. 12:10; John 19:34, 37).

23. Darkness over the land (Amos 8:9; Matt. 27:45).

24. Buried in a rich man's tomb (Isa. 53:9; Matt. 27:57-60).

Someone with a mathematical turn of mind has figured out that by the laws of compound probability there was only one chance in 33,554,432 that these prophesied events could have happened accidentally! Surely here is proof that the Bible is the very Word of God. Here also is clear demonstration that the death of Christ on the cross was God's ordained way to bring about the salvation of sinners.

4. **Predictions of His resurrection and ascension.** Neither history nor prophecy leaves God's Messiah dead, in a tomb. Read such prophecies as

Psalm 16:10 and 110:1 together with their application in Acts 2:23 to 36, and it is clear why Paul could say, ". . . he rose again the third day according to the scriptures" (I Cor. 15:4).

SUMMARY

God foretold in great detail the coming of His Messiah, as a suffering Saviour and as a glorious King.

Many of these predictions were exactly and literally fulfilled at the first coming of Christ.

The key by which we can understand the Old Testament prophecies and the New Testament Gospel records is the *time* element. Some of the details prophesied of the Messiah were postponed until a second coming.

The messianic prophecies already fulfilled are a guarantee of the fact and of the literal nature of the ones yet to be fulfilled when Christ comes again.

3

Second Coming of Christ:
Rapture . . . Phase One

SUGGESTED BACKGROUND DEVOTIONAL READING

Monday—The Meeting in the Air (I Thess. 4:13-18)
Tuesday—Whether We Wake or Sleep (I Thess. 5:1-11)
Wednesday—We Shall Be Changed (I Cor. 15:50-58)
Thursday—Received unto Christ (John 14:1-6)
Friday—Waiting for God's Son (I Thess. 1:1-10)
Saturday—The Blessed Hope (Titus 2:1-14)
Sunday—Made Like Him (Phil. 3:20-21; I John 3:1-3)

INTRODUCTION

As we have seen in the previous chapters, the central theme of prophecy is the prediction of the coming of God's Messiah, God's Saviour, into the world. The next two chapters follow this theme one step further and deal with His second coming. Since the first coming has already taken place but the second coming has not, in our present study we step for the first time into the realm of unfulfilled prophecy. This will begin our study of "future events."

THE AIM

The primary aim of this chapter is to get persons to look for, to expect, to eagerly anticipate the coming of Christ. This blessed hope should be made a means of encouragement and comfort to the believers and a challenge to them to be ready to meet Him. To the unsaved it should be a timely warning that their day of salvation will not last forever, that they need to accept Him now as their Saviour in order to be ready to share in that blessed hope.

THE DEVELOPMENT

First, we need to show why there must be a second coming; why all of the prophecies of the Messiah were not fulfilled the first time He came.

Second, we should note the way prophecy unfolds as time goes on, bringing out into clear distinction details which formerly were undistinguishable.

Third, we shall study I Thessalonians 4:13-18, the main passage of Scripture which deals with the first aspect of the second coming, which we call the "Rapture." In it we shall see the course of events which will take place at the Rapture, the persons involved, and the outcome of it.

Fourth, we shall turn to I Corinthians 15:51-54, the second great Scripture passage dealing with the Rapture, to learn two additional details.

THE EXPOSITION

I. Why a Second Coming Was Necessary

Very simply, there needs to be a second coming of Christ because at the first coming only a small part of the prophecies concerning Him and His work were accomplished. We have pointed out before that the Old Testament shows two general lines of prophecy, one that pictures a lowly, suffering servant dying for the sins of others, the other that pictures Him as a mighty and glorious king reigning in justice and peace over the whole world. When Jesus came the first time, He fulfilled the first picture. But He himself promised that He would come again, the next time in power and glory to complete the other part of the picture.

But why didn't He fulfill all the first time? A careful study of the gospel records, particularly of Matthew, will reveal that Jesus at the beginning of His ministry offered himself to the nation of Israel as their promised Messiah and announced that the prophesied kingdom was at hand. But as their opposition grew and it became clear that they were not going to accept Him, He began to teach them of His suffering and death, and of the building of a new thing, the church. He prepared them for a long delay, a postponement in the setting up of His glorious kingdom. And He promised He would come again, the next time in power and glory, to reign.

Of course, this was no surprise to God. He knew ahead what their response would be. But it brought about His purpose that Christ must first suffer and afterward enter into His glory.

II. The Unfolding of Prophecy

An important principle of prophecy is illustrated here. The Old Testament prophets had simply told of the coming of a Messiah. Many details were given, but their relationship to each other was not clearly seen. However, in the New Testament this coming is seen to unfold into two comings. Both these comings were foreseen and foretold in the Old Testament, but they could not be distinguished until the time key was found.

In much the same way there is a further unfolding of prophecy in the New Testament. In the Gospels Jesus very clearly and emphatically says that He is coming again. Once more many details are given, but their relationship to each other is not clearly seen. However, when we come to the writings of the Apostle Paul, this second coming of Christ unfolds again into two parts. First He will come again *for* His saints, to rapture them out of this world before that terrible time of judgment called the "Great Tribulation." Then, after that tribulation, He will return *with* His saints to set up His kingdom and to reign as the prophets foretold. The first aspect of His second coming is usually referred to by the term "Rapture." The second aspect of His second coming is frequently called the "Revelation."

When a traveler approaches the great Rocky Mountain range from across our western prairies, he first sees a number of peaks, or mountains which appear to be all lined up in an even row across the horizon. They all appear to be the same distance away. But as he comes closer and reaches one of these peaks, he sees that this is not the case. Two peaks that appeared to be side by side are seen to be a long way apart, perhaps with a valley between and many lesser peaks not seen at all from a distance.

So it is in prophecy. The prophets looked ahead and saw many details about the coming Messiah. From their vantage point these all appeared to be together. But when time passed and history reached the first peak, the first coming of Christ, it then became clear that there was another peak away beyond, a second coming. In between was a great valley unseen before, the age of the church, our present dispensation. Also, looking again from our new vantage point, the next peak is seen to be actually a twin peak, with two parts, the Rapture and the Revelation.

III. The Primary Scripture Passage on the Rapture (I Thess. 4:13-18)

This first phase of the second coming of Christ is referred to frequently in the New Testament, but this passage especially gives us a clear and detailed presentation of it.

1. **The persons involved** (vv. 14-15). Two groups of persons are mentioned. The first group is called in verses 13 and 15 "them which are asleep," in verse 14 "them also which sleep in Jesus," and in verse 16 "the dead in Christ." The term "sleep" is a term used in the Bible to describe the death of the believer (cf. John 11:11-13), a term which sounds less harsh and serves to soften the rude shock of the word "death." Evidently the Thessalonian Christians had become concerned about those of their group who had died, wondering whether this would cut them off from participation in the blessed hope which Paul had taught them to expect. He had given them instruction regarding the coming of Christ, and they were waiting for the Son of God to come from heaven to receive them to himself. But while they were waiting some of their number died. They hadn't expected this; they must have thought: "Too bad, they won't be here when Jesus comes." Now Paul writes to reassure them. The ones who have fallen asleep in Jesus will certainly not miss out. The Rapture will include them.

The second group involved in the Rapture is mentioned in verses 15 and 17, "we which are alive and remain." That means that when Jesus comes back, there will be believers alive here on the earth. This is not some mysterious event off in the dim future of eternity somewhere. It belongs to time, to history, to this world. Right now there are these two groups, the living saints and the saints who have died in Christ. If Christ should come today, we should be among those who are alive and remain. If He tarries His coming, we may fall asleep in Jesus. But the Rapture, whenever it comes, will include us all.

There is no hint here of a partial Rapture. Some teach that only *some* of the believers living when Jesus comes will be taken up to meet Him: those who are purified, or those who are looking for Him, or those who are ready. But our salvation does not depend on our purity or our watchfulness or our readiness. It depends only on His faithfulness, And I believe the Scriptures teach that when this blessed event comes, all the saved will go up to be with their Lord.

Some unbelievers have used this passage to raise an objection to the whole doctrine of the second coming. They say this verse teaches that Paul was expecting Jesus to come in his day; he said, "*We* who are alive and remain." Since Jesus did not come in Paul's day, Paul was wrong. And if he was wrong about that, he was wrong also about the whole idea of Christ's coming again. But their blind, unbelieving minds do not see that Paul would have been wrong if he had *not* been expecting Jesus to come in his day. Jesus had commanded him to watch and be ready, because he did not know, was not supposed to know, when Jesus would come. He did not say, "I know Jesus is coming back while I am still alive." He merely expressed his expectation and hope that he would be among those who were alive and remained unto the coming of the Lord. And in doing that he was right, not wrong.

2. **The main event** (v. 16). "For the Lord himself shall descend from heaven." This is the glorious event, the great moment, we have been longing for. From that time in the Upper Room when Jesus said, "If I go . . . I will come again, and receive you unto myself" (John 14:3), this has been the blessed hope of the believer. The angels at the Ascension repeated it (Acts 1:11). Again and again Paul calls it to mind as a challenge and impetus to our duties (I Cor. 1:7; Phil. 3:20-21; Col. 3:4, and many more). Every chapter of this little letter to the Thessalonians reechoes it. Every New Testament writer calls attention to it. Down through the ages it has gladdened the heart and quickened the step of God's people.

Jesus is coming again! Let each of us ask ourselves at this point: Have I been looking for Him? Am I ready to meet Him? Have I been living and working as if I expected Him soon? The study of prophecy is worse than useless if it doesn't bring us face to face with this One, and this event, which is the center of all prophecy.

3. **The accompanying circumstances** (v. 16). Three things are said to accompany His appearance, to mark this event. Christ will descend from heaven "with a shout, with the voice of the archangel, and with the trump of God."

Here we need to be very careful how we handle the prophetic Word. We need to remember what we learned in an earlier chapter. Prophecy is a lamp shining in a dark place. It is not a sun that dispels all darkness. It does not answer all questions. In fact, it often lets us see just enough to raise even more questions. And often the answers to these questions must await the coming of the day. Perhaps in these phrases, we are dealing with a part of the picture which we cannot at present fully explain. If that is the case, it ought not to trouble us.

Are these three to be considered as three distinct events separate from each other, and each bearing its own explanation? Some have tried to understand it so, but they have not been very successful in demonstrating it. Or, are these three expressions to be understood as describing one event? When Jesus comes, He will announce His arrival and call forth His people with a shout. This shout will be the voice of the archangel and will assemble the saints as the trumpet used to assemble the congregation of old. Perhaps this is the simpler explanation, at least until we can know more about it.

"With a shout." The word here in the original suggests a shout of command, the loud, sharp order of an officer to his troops. Some have seen here a parallel to John 11:43, when Jesus cried for Lazarus to come forth from the tomb, and thus refer it to the resurrection of the dead which takes place at this time. But there a different word is used, and perhaps it is better to preserve the military significance of this command-shout.

"With the voice of the archangel." Only one archangel is named in the Bible, Michael (Jude 9). According to the Old Testament prophetic book Daniel (10:21; 12:1), Michael is especially the "prince which standeth for the children of thy people," that is, for Israel. So the voice of the arch-angel here suggests that this is an event of great significance to Israel, perhaps the proclamation that the parenthetic Church Age is past and God is again dealing with His people Israel.

"With the trump of God." In the Scriptures the trumpet was used for two functions. First, a trumpet called together the convocation of Israel for the worship of the Lord, and the trumpet along with other instruments of music sounded forth the praise of the Lord in the temple worship (Num. 10:2, 9). Second, the trumpet was used to call forth God's armies to war. Recall the fall of Jericho as the people marched around the city and the priests blew the trumpets (Joshua 6:4), or the story of Gideon (Judges 7:16). Joel (2:1) prophesied, "Blow ye the trumpet in Zion . . . for the day of the Lord cometh." In the New Testament Paul speaks of the trumpet as a signal for war (I Cor. 14:8). And in the Book of Revelation the seven trumpets seem to be God's declaration of war and destruction against the unbelieving earth dwellers of the end time.

So, all three of these circumstances which accompany the descent of the Lord from heaven seem to have a military significance. They suggest that there is a stern aspect to the coming. Along with the blessed prospects which it brings to those who are in Christ, it is also the grim proclamation of war on the unbelieving world, and of terrible trouble upon God's people of Israel. It is the signal that the Great Tribulation is to begin; the great judgment of the terrible Day of the Lord is at hand.

4. **The events which occur.** Three tremendous events will transpire when the Lord comes. We are told that "the dead in Christ shall rise first" (v. 16). Of the two groups involved in this great event, Paul says that the ones who are alive and remain will not precede, will not go ahead of, those that are asleep. Rather, the dead in Christ will rise first.

When a believer dies, his body is laid in the grave, but his spirit goes to be with his Lord in heaven. This is the clear teaching of the New Testament. When Christ comes at the Rapture, the souls of those believers who have died will come along with Him (v. 14). And the first great event of that Rapture will be the resurrection of those dead in Christ. Their bodies will come forth from their graves; their spirits will be reunited with their resurrected, glorified bodies; and as whole, completely saved persons, body, soul, and spirit, they will share in this great occasion. This is the wonderful prospect the New Testament always holds out as the blessed hope of those who die in the Lord. "Wherefore comfort one another with these words" (v. 18; cf. v. 14). This is the first resurrection, the resurrection of the just, those that are Christ's at His coming.

The second group involved, those who are alive when Jesus comes, will also undergo a marvelous experience. But Paul tells of this in another passage. Here he is speaking primarily of those who sleep. For them the coming of Christ will mean resurrection, restoration to life again in the body.

The third event will be the catching up of all the saved to meet the Lord in the air. This is the action which gives us the name "Rapture" for this first aspect of the second coming of Christ. The word does not occur in our English Bibles; it comes from the Latin and means "caught up," or "snatched up." Christ is coming to snatch us out of the world and carry us away to be with himself.

We shall all be caught up "together," both the dead in Christ who have now been resurrected, and those who are living when He comes. Together we go up to meet the Lord. Here is the reunion with our loved ones which brings comfort to our hearts when our loved ones are taken from us in death. We shall meet them again, when together we are caught up in the Rapture.

We shall "meet the Lord in the air." It is clear from other prophetic teaching that this is a coming of the Lord especially for His own. Having met us in the air, He returns to heaven with us for some other prophesied events. Later will take place the other aspect of the second coming in power and glory. Then His feet will stand on the Mount of Olives. This first time He comes into the air to catch us away to be with himself.

5. **The blessed results** (vv. 17-18). Two wonderful truths are called to our attention as Paul closes this illuminating glimpse of the Rapture. First, he declares that "so shall we ever be with the Lord." Of course, he says this from the vantage point of the living, for the dead in Christ have been with Him since the moment they died. But for the living this is the first meeting with their Lord, and the guarantee of this verse is that it will never end. Jesus' precious promise to the sorrowing disciples was, "I will come again, and receive you unto myself, that where I am, there ye may be also" (John 14:3). To be with Jesus will be the choicest blessing that heaven can afford. Think of it!

The second wonderful truth is found in verse 18. Right now, even before that wonderful day comes, there is inexpressible comfort to be found in contemplating these truths. This passage began with the concern of the living for their loved ones who had fallen asleep in Jesus. This precious promise was given to comfort them, that they sorrow not as others who had no hope. Almost everyone has felt the sorrow of losing loved ones. Here is comfort for such an experience. Comfort now, and glory later—that is what the Rapture, the coming of Christ for His own, means to us.

IV. Additional Details Regarding the Rapture

Before we can close our study of this great prophecy, we need to look at one more important passage. I Corinthians 15:51-54. It is part of the great resurrection chapter, in which Paul discusses the certainty of Christ's resurrection and of ours, the order of the resurrection, and the nature of the resurrection body. The dead must be raised with a new, glorified, incorruptible body. But "we shall not all sleep," so before he closes this exposition of the doctrine of resurrection, he must explain what will be the experience of those who are living when Jesus comes. For they, too, must have that glorified, new body. How will they get it?

1. **The living saints will be transformed.** Twice Paul says it: "We shall all be changed" (vv. 51-52). He describes the transformation by saying that "this corruptible [body] must put on incorruption, and this mortal [body] must put on immortality." Just as the dead will be raised incorruptible, so the living will be changed into incorruptibility. In other words, a change will take place in the living saints by which they will receive the same incorruptible, glorious bodies the dead receive by resurrection.

Summarizing then, when the Lord comes in the Rapture, three things will happen. First, the dead in Christ will be resurrected in their glorified bodies. Second, the living saints will be transformed without dying into the same glorified bodies. And third, they all together will be caught up in the clouds to meet the Lord in the air.

2. **All this will happen in an instant.** Paul says, "In a moment, in the twinkling of an eye." It is difficult to see how he could have made it clearer. One of these days, at a time when there are believers living here in the flesh, as now, the signal will be given. The Lord will descend, the shout of command will be given, the last trumpet will blow. And instantaneously, without warning or anticipation, without a second for preparation or last-minute repentance, the resurrection of the dead and the transformation of the living will usher the saints into the presence of their Lord. That same instant will introduce the unsaved world into the final, terrible days of God's wrath on His enemies.

Not a single prophecy or sign still needs to be fulfilled before that instant arrives. The Rapture, the first aspect of the second coming of Christ, is the next event of prophecy.

SUMMARY

Christ came once. He will come again to complete His prophesied work.

Christ's second coming will consist of two stages. First, He will come to get His saved ones and take them to himself.

This Rapture will include both living and dead in their glorified bodies.

4

Second Coming of Christ: Revelation . . . Phase Two

INTRODUCTION

In the last chapter we saw how prophetic Scripture unfolds as we study through the Bible. In the Old Testament the promise was, "Messiah is coming." In the Gospels this unfolds into two comings, and the promise is, "Jesus is coming again." In Paul's epistles this second coming unfolds into two aspects. First, He is coming to catch away His saints—the Rapture. Second, He is coming in power and glory to set up His kingdom. This second aspect of Christ's second coming is our study in this chapter.

THE AIM

A natural curiosity gathers about this event and its attendant circumstances. Men want to know how human history is going to come out ultimately, how and when the end of the world will come. But remember that our purpose in this study is not to satisfy curiosity, but to see the significance of prophetic truth to our own spiritual needs. Our central purpose therefore is to show that Jesus Christ, and His second advent, is the goal of all human history, God's perfect and final answer to the world and all its needs.

38

THE DEVELOPMENT

First, we will show the *certainty* of this coming, running through the Bible to show that this is one of the greatest themes of prophetic truth.

Second, we will consider the *significance* of this coming.

Third, we will deal very briefly with the *time* of Christ's coming.

THE EXPOSITION

I. The Certainty of His Coming

The second coming of Christ in power and glory is just as certain as the Word of God is true. There may be those who claim to believe the Bible who do not accept this teaching, but if so, they are either ignorant or inconsistent or unbelievers. Anyone who will simply read the Bible for himself will quickly acknowledge that it teaches this truth most clearly and positively.

1. **It is the major theme of all Old Testament messianic prophecy.** We have seen in previous chapters that the Old Testament prophesied the coming of a Messiah from God to save His people and the world, and that this prophetic picture presented His coming in two roles, as a suffering Saviour and as a glorious King. We have traced some of the prophecies of His humiliation, all fulfilled in His first coming.

But by far the larger part of that Old Testament picture was devoted to His coming in glory and power to destroy His enemies and to establish God's kingdom among men. These are the prophecies to be fulfilled at His second coming. We can trace only a few of them here.

Messianic prophecy began at the very start of the human race. The first promise of God that He would send a man to save the human family from the curse of sin (Gen. 3:15) contains in seed form a suggestion of the first coming of Christ (Satan would bruise His heel), and the second coming (the woman's seed would bruise Satan's head).

Turn next to Genesis 49:10: "The sceptre shall not depart from Judah, nor a lawgiver from between his feet, until Shiloh come; and unto him shall the gathering of the people be." The precise significance of the term "Shiloh" may be questioned, but there is no question that it is a reference to the Messiah. Both the Jewish and Christian interpretations have so understood it. And its reference to the scepter and the lawgiver applies it to the ruling, reigning ministry of the Messiah, which belongs to His second coming.

Come down to the time of David and the passages begin to multiply. God promises to David that He will establish his house and that his throne will endure forever; he will never lack a son to sit upon his throne (II Sam. 7:12-17; cf. Jer. 33:17). The Messianic Psalms for the most part refer to the second advent of Messiah and to His kingdom. In Psalm 2 God introduces His Son as His chosen King in spite of the conspiracy of the kings of the earth against His Anointed. Psalm 24 is a welcome-song to greet the arrival at Jerusalem of the "King of glory." Psalm 45 is a beautiful wedding song of that King, and the majesty, glory and blessing of His reign are described in dazzling splendor. Psalm 50 informs us that it is God himself who is coming, and teaches the deity of the coming Messiah. Psalm 69, which chiefly pictures the sufferings of Messiah at His first advent, yet closes with a promise which is to be fulfilled when He comes again: "For God will save Zion, and will build the cities of Judah." Psalm 72 is a beautiful description of the blessedness of the millennial kingdom, when Christ is reigning and the world acknowledges His leadership. Psalm 110 shows Christ sitting at the right hand of God, waiting until God shall make His enemies His footstool; then He will rule in the day of His power.

Isaiah is full of references to the glories of Messiah's kingdom and coming. Isaiah 2:1-5 foretells the time when all nations will flow into the mountain of the Lord's house, and they will beat their swords into plowshares and their spears into pruninghooks and will learn war no more. Chapter 9, verses 6 and 7, speaks of the birth of a child, the giving of a son, one called "Wonderful, Counsellor, The mighty God, The everlasting Father, The Prince of Peace," upon whose shoulder shall be the government, upon the throne of David forever. In 26:20 and 21 this coming one is again identified with the Lord himself. Chapters 32 to 35 intertwine with the judgments many clear references to the glories of His kingdom and the blessings He will bring when He comes (35:4). Chapter 40 breaks out with the cry, "Prepare ye the way of the Lord" (v. 3). "The glory of the Lord shall be revealed" (v. 5). "Behold, the Lord God will come with strong hand, and his arm shall rule for him" (v. 10). "He shall feed his flock like a shepherd" (v. 11). The servant of the Lord who was wounded for our transgressions and suffered vicariously for the sins of man (chap.

53) is also the servant who "shall bring forth judgment to the Gentiles . . . and the isles shall wait for his law" (cf. 42:1-4). Isaiah 59:20 says, "The Redeemer shall come to Zion," and the next chapter tells of the elaborate welcome He will receive from the Gentiles who want to acknowledge His rule. Jesus read from Isaiah 61 in the synagogue of Nazareth, but stopped in the middle of a sentence. The part which followed speaks of the glories of His second advent and was not appropriate then, but will be when He comes again. And after a terrible vision of this coming King sprinkled with the blood of His enemies in chapter 63, Isaiah brings his book to a close with the fervent prayer, "Oh that thou wouldest rend the heavens, that thou wouldest come down" (64:1), and God's solemn promise, "Behold, the Lord will come" to render His anger upon His enemies and His blessings upon His people (66:15).

Jeremiah breaks the monotony of his messages of doom on the wicked city of Jerusalem to bring us this prophecy: "Behold, the days come, saith the Lord, that I will raise unto David a righteous Branch, and a King shall reign and prosper, and shall execute judgment and justice in the earth. In his days Judah shall be saved, and Israel shall dwell safely: and this is his name whereby he shall be called, THE LORD OUR RIGHTEOUSNESS" (Jer. 23:5-6).

Ezekiel also speaks from the midst of Israel's sin and captivity. His message in the first part is primarily one of judgment, with a few comforting promises of restoration. For example, in 34:23-25 he says, "I will set up one shepherd over them, and he shall feed them, even my servant David. . . . And I the Lord will be their God, and my servant David a prince among them. . . . And I will make with them a covenant of peace. . . ." And after the famous vision of the valley of dry bones Ezekiel goes on to explain, "I will take the children of Israel from among the heathen, whither they be gone, and will gather them on every side, and bring them into their own land: and I will make them one nation in the land . . . and one king shall be king to them all. . . . And David my servant shall be king over them; and they all shall have one shepherd: they shall also walk in my judgments. . . . And they shall dwell in the land . . . for ever: and my servant David shall be their prince for ever" (37:21-25). In the latter part of his book, which describes the temple yet to be built by the restored nation, he speaks much of this "prince."

Daniel uses the figure of a stone "cut out without hands" (2:34) to describe the dramatic destruction of Gentile world power when the God of heaven sets up His kingdom, and identifies this figure as the Son of man (7:13-14), a title which Jesus preferred above all others to refer to himself.

Hosea looks forward to a future day when "the children of Israel [shall] return, and seek the Lord their God, and David their king" (3:5). Joel prophesies, "The Lord also shall roar out of Zion . . . the Lord will be the hope of his people. . . . So shall ye know that I am the Lord your God *dwelling in Zion,* my holy mountain" (3:16-17). Amos foresees, "In that day will I raise up the tabernacle of David that is fallen . . . and I will build it as in the days of old" (9:11). Obadiah says, "Upon mount Zion shall be deliverance, and there shall be holiness; and the house of Jacob shall possess their possessions. . . . and the kingdom shall be the Lord's" (vv. 17, 21). Micah follows his solemn prediction that Jerusalem will be plowed as a field (3:12) with the promise of a future time when the law will go forth out of Zion, when all nations will dwell in peace (4:1-7), then reveals that out of Bethlehem "shall he come forth unto me that is to be ruler in Israel" (5:2). Zephaniah paints a dark picture of the coming day of the Lord, but closes with a song of praise: "The Lord hath taken away thy judgments . . . the king of Israel, even the Lord, is in the midst of thee: thou shalt not see evil any more" (3:14-17).

Zechariah tells of one called "The Branch" who will be "a priest upon his throne" (cf. 6:12-13). He foresees the public entry of Christ into the city of Jerusalem: "Thy King cometh unto thee: he is just, and having salvation; lowly, and riding upon an ass"; but he sees a further time when that king "shall speak peace unto the heathen: and his dominion shall be from sea even to sea" (9:9-10). He predicts the time when the inhabitants of Jerusalem will look upon the One whom they pierced and will mourn for Him (12:10). He sees Jerusalem surrounded by her enemies, then says, "His feet shall stand in that day upon the mount of Olives" (14:4), and proceeds to tell of the destruction of those enemies and the establishment of Messiah's kingdom over all the earth.

These are a few of the prophecies of the Old Testament which look forward to the second coming of Christ in power and glory.

2. **It is the major theme of New Testament prophecy as well.** When the angel announced to Mary that she should become the mother of this

wonderful Messiah, he told her, "He shall be great, and shall be called the Son of the Highest: and the Lord God shall give unto him the throne of his father David: and he shall reign over the house of Jacob for ever; and of his kingdom there shall be no end" (Luke 1:32-33).

Jesus encouraged His disciples with the promise that they would share with Him "in the regeneration when the Son of man shall sit in the throne of his glory" (Matt. 19:28). Later when He stood in judgment before the high priest and was placed under oath to tell the truth about himself, He affirmed His messianic identity and then prophesied to that representative of the Jewish nation, "Hereafter shall ye see the Son of man sitting on the right hand of power, and coming in the clouds of heaven" (Matt. 26:64).

The rest of the New Testament bears throughout the same impression. The resurrected Jesus asked His confused disciples, "Ought not Christ to have suffered these things, and to enter into his glory?" (Luke 24:26). As He was taken up into heaven, the angelic promise was, "this same Jesus . . . shall so come in like manner as ye have seen him go into heaven" (Acts 1:11). The early preaching in the Book of Acts exhorted the people of Jerusalem to repent and be converted, speaking of the time "when the times of refreshing shall come from the presence of the Lord; and he shall send Jesus Christ . . . whom the heaven must receive until the times of restitution of all things, which God hath spoken by the mouth of all his holy prophets since the world began" (Acts 3:19-21).

Paul often in his letters uses this great prophetic truth to encourage or to challenge his readers. In II Thessalonians 1:7-10, one of his earliest letters, he assures the troubled and suffering believers that they will have "rest with us, when the Lord Jesus shall be revealed from heaven with his mighty angels, in flaming fire taking vengeance . . . when he shall come to be glorified in his saints. . . ." In I Timothy 6:13-16, one of his last letters, he exhorts this young minister to faithfulness "until the appearing of our Lord Jesus Christ: which in his times he shall shew, who is the blessed and only Potentate, the King of kings, and Lord of lords; who only hath immortality. . . ."

James exhorts to patience in view of the fact that "the coming of the Lord draweth nigh. . . . The judge standeth before the door" (James 5:7-9). Peter warns that this doctrine will be the special object of scoffing in the last days, but emphatically declares, "The day of the Lord will come" (II Peter 3:3-4, 8-10, 12, 14). Jude quotes a prophecy, otherwise unknown, from the lips of Enoch back before the Flood: "Behold, the Lord cometh with ten thousands of his saints, to execute judgment upon all . . ." (Jude 14-15). And John opens his Book of Revelation with the key words, "Behold, he cometh with clouds; and every eye shall see him" (1:7), then goes on to make this great event the climax and focal point of his entire book.

Certainly, there can be no doubt. The whole Bible teaches that Jesus Christ is coming again.

II. The Significance of His Coming

1. **It will mean the climax and culmination of human history**. One of the great blessings of the Christian faith is the way it gives meaning and purpose to history. The unbelieving world has been so deceived by its evolutionary and atheistic philosophy that it can see no reason, no direction, to the events of today, nor even of yesterday, let alone of the future. The Bible reveals God's purposes and traces in broad outline the course in which He is directing history. According to Bible prophecy, the goal and accomplishment of all God's purposes for the human race will be realized in the second coming of Christ.

This is clearly seen in the place it occupies in the prophetic Scriptures of the Old Testament. The prophets saw God working in human history. They traced His dealing and guidance in the past, they rebuked and warned of His concern over present failures, and they promised His ultimate consummation. Their enlightened eyes saw more clearly than others man's utter failure in every realm: political, social, economic, physical, moral, spiritual. They attached no vain hope to man's ability to improve himself, and their prophecies do not anticipate a gradual upward trend. Rather, man has had his day and has demonstrated his utter failure. Soon God will step in and have His day. "The day of the Lord" will come. The historic kingdom which failed so miserably because of the faults of David and his sons will soon give way to the messianic kingdom of David's greater Son who will not fail. The golden age to come will be a time when all the areas of human experience will have opportunity for perfect development—a perfect government, a righteous society, a just economy, a physical world without a curse, a right moral standard perfectly administered, a spiritual and ecclesiastical system directly regulated by God himself. And all these wonderful accomplishments will be the work of God's Messiah. History will find its meaning and its goal when the Lord Jesus Christ comes again in power and glory to set up His kingdom and to run the world as it ought to be run.

The central significance of this climactic event as the culmination of history is reflected in the very word used to identify it. We call it the Revelation, to distinguish it from the Rapture. This word is a scriptural title, used very frequently in the New Testament to refer to this event, often when the English versions do not make this clear. The word means an uncovering, an unveiling, a making plain, a manifestation. It reflects a situation in which God, His ways, His kingdom, His people, and His purposes have not been clearly seen or understood but now in this event are opened up to plain view. The world has been going through a dark night. Sin and Satan have been blinding the eyes of them that believe not. God and righteousness have been real only to the eyes of faith. But the morning cometh. God's King will be revealed, manifested, unveiled, made plainly visible. This is the Revelation of Jesus Christ, when He comes not secretly to snatch away His church, but openly to exercise all His divine power and authority to rule the world.

Christian, take courage! It will not always be dark. We will not always be the underdog. The world will not always laugh at us. One of these days Jesus Christ will be revealed; the truth will be out; things will appear in their proper perspective. Then it will all be worthwhile, won't it?

2. **It will mean the judgment of sin and the doom of sinners**. This has been implied in much that has already been said, but it needs to be made very specific. The second coming of Christ is not all blessing and good. It has also a terrible side, as it affects sin and sinners.

The Old Testament foresaw this aspect of Messiah's coming. In Malachi 3:1-6 the people were eagerly anticipating the coming of Messiah to free them from their yoke of bondage to foreign powers and bring them into the glorious kingdom. But the prophet warns them. To paraphrase his words, he says something like this: "Yes, he is coming all right. But who is going to be able to endure his coming? When he comes he will judge sin, he will be a fire to burn out the dross, he will be a strong soap to clean out the filth, he will utterly destroy all sin. You see, he hasn't changed. He still hates sin, and when he comes he will destroy it. In the light of this, do you still want him to come?" Now look at Malachi 4:1 and 2. Messiah's coming will mean burning and destruction to the sinner. But to those who fear the Lord it will be the rising of a sun whose rays bring healing and blessing.

The New Testament also emphasizes this aspect of Christ's second coming. One of the chief passages in the New Testament referring to this second aspect of Christ's second coming is II Thessalonians 2:1-12. Paul writes to clear up a confusion. Some were saying that the day of the Lord had already come. Paul insists that two events must come first, (1) the apostasy and (2) the revealing of the Antichrist, the man of sin. Particularly he deals with this second point. He points out the Antichrist cannot come until that which restrains is taken out of the way. Today sin is being held back from its full culmination by the "salt of the earth"—the church, or the Holy Spirit in the church. But when the Rapture takes place and the restraint is removed, then sin will quickly ripen into its final manifestation in the man of sin, the Antichrist. Now note especially what is to happen to this Antichrist: "Whom the Lord shall consume with the spirit of his mouth, and shall destroy with the brightness of his coming" (v. 8).

But this passage teaches more than the end of the man of sin. It also pronounces an eternal damnation upon every person who has refused to receive the Gospel. There will be no second chance after the Rapture for those who have refused Christ before it. Those who "received not" and "believed not" (vv. 10, 12, *past* tenses) will receive from God "strong delusion," judicial blindness, that they should believe the lie of Antichrist and be damned.

3. **It will mean the personal triumph and vindication of Christ**. Try to imagine what these years of humiliation and suffering must mean to our blessed Lord. "When he was reviled, [he] reviled not again; when he suffered, he threatened not; but committed himself to him that judgeth righteously" (I Peter 2:23). That righteous judgment of God has waited long. Our Lord is still maligned, cursed, hated, despised, rejected of evil men. But, praise God! It will not wait forever. One of these days the heavens will open and Christ will ride forth, not this time to shame and reproach, but to glory and recognition, resplendent with all the titles that are His by right. The climax of all the ages is in Revelation 19:11-21. As we read it again, let us join the voices in heaven as they shout, "Alleluia:

for the Lord God omnipotent reigneth. ... The kingdoms of this world are become the kingdoms of our Lord, and of his Christ; and he shall reign for ever and ever."

III. The Time of His Coming

We will consider only three general observations on this important subject.

1. **The time of Christ's second coming is a secret** which God has chosen to leave unrevealed. It is not known, it cannot be figured out, and it will never be known until it actually transpires. Much harm has been done the teaching of this precious doctrine of the second coming by misguided and unbelieving attempts to set dates. (Read Matt. 24:36, 42, 44; Mark 13:32; Luke 12:39-40; Acts 1:7; I Thess. 5:1-2, 6.)

2. **The Bible does give us many signs** which warn us that the time of His coming is drawing near. This is a whole subject in itself, one which we will include in a later chapter. When we speak of signs, however, we need to recognize that all signs have to do with this second aspect of Christ's second coming, not with the Rapture of the church. There are no signs of the Rapture. But since the Rapture comes first, by seven years, then when we see signs that the later event is getting close we may be sure that the preceding one is even nearer.

3. **The second aspect of Christ's coming, the Revelation, differs from the first aspect, the Rapture**, in that there are events which must precede it, whereas the Rapture is imminent—it may happen at any moment. There is not a single prophesied event, not a single sign, which the Bible puts between our own time and the Rapture. Christ's coming to take us to himself is the next item on the prophetic calendar. We are waiting, hoping, looking for Him to come. It may be today. When that blessed event has taken place, then prophetic Scripture outlines a series of events which will lead up to the glorious appearing of Christ in power and glory. But we are not looking for the Antichrist, or for the tribulation, or for the return of Israel, or for an invasion of Palestine, or for a ten-kingdom development. We are looking for our Lord. The next sound we hear may be His voice, calling forth the sleeping saints. The next sensation we experience may be a strange transformation in these physical bodies as we exchange cor-

ruptibility for incorruptibility. The next journey we take may be upward. The next face we see may be the face of our wonderful Lord!

Even so, come, Lord Jesus!

SUMMARY

Jesus is coming again to this earth—actually, literally, really.

His coming will mean that this world will finally realize the goal and purpose which God intended for it, with perfect righteousness, peace, justice, perfectly administered by the only man who has the right to rule, Christ, the King of kings and Lord of lords.

It will mean the end of sin and the doom of sinners.

We do not know when Christ is coming, but we do know that we must be ready at any moment. All indications are that He is coming soon.

5

The Jew:
His Land in Prophecy

**SUGGESTED
BACKGROUND
DEVOTIONAL
READING**

Monday—Abraham (Gen. 12:1-3; 13:14-17; 17:4-8)
Tuesday—God's Promise to Moses (Deut. 4:23-40)
Wednesday—A Remnant Preserved (Rom. 11:1-10)
Thursday—A Restoration Assured (Rom. 11:11-32)
Friday—From All Nations (Jer. 23:5-8; Hosea 3:4-5)
Saturday—A New Heart To Be Given (Ezek. 36:16-28)
Sunday—The Dry Bones Will Live (Ezek. 37:1-14)

INTRODUCTION

Once when Frederick the Great asked for a proof of the Bible in one word, the answer given was "The Jew!" Truly the Jewish nation is the wonder of the ages: the past's greatest prodigy, the present's greatest puzzle, and the future's greatest proof. The nation of Israel figures so largely in Biblical prophecy that no study of this subject can ignore it, and no system of interpretation can be correct if it errs at this point.

THE AIM

The primary purpose of this chapter is to come to an understanding of the place which the Jewish people occupy in God's program. To do this it will be necessary to look at the past and present as well as the future. But this is only the first purpose. There must also be another. The second purpose is to encourage a proper attitude toward the Jew in the hearts and actions of Christians. Therefore, as you study this chapter, pray that the Holy Spirit will open your eyes and give you a special understanding of and love for the Jew.

THE DEVELOPMENT

First, we shall review the two great promises or covenants God made to

Israel in which He stated clearly His eternal purpose for their nation.

Second, we shall trace very briefly the way these covenants have actually worked out in the history of the Jews.

Third, we shall consider the all-important question: Is God through with the Jew? Has Israel been set aside by God? The answer will be found in a study of Romans 11.

Fourth, we shall look at what prophecy says about the present situation of the Jews in their dispersion among the nations.

Fifth, we shall outline the future prospect of Israel as foretold in Scripture.

THE EXPOSITION

I. God's Two Promises to Israel

The Old Testament clearly speaks of the nation of Israel as God's chosen people. God is the God of Abraham, Isaac and Jacob. The Jews occupied a special place in God's dealings with men. This place of privilege was theirs because God picked them out and blessed them. Two distinct promises, or covenants, marked this relationship.

1. **The promise to Abraham** (Gen. 12:1-3, 7; 13:14-17; 17:4-8). The story of the Chosen People begins with this sovereign act of God's grace, when He called Abraham and gave him this promise. The promise included a posterity which would become a great nation, a seed who would bring blessing to the whole earth, divine protection and special privilege, and the land of Palestine to be their land. This promise was to last forever (13:15; 17:7-8). God repeated it to Abraham on several occasions, confirming it with solemn ritual and by miraculous accomplishment. He reaffirmed it with Isaac and then with Jacob. Throughout the Old Testament God is pleased to call attention to His own faithfulness by reminding His people that He is a covenant-keeping God who remembers the promise He made to Abraham.

Especially for our purpose here, it must be noted that this was an unconditional promise, no strings attached! God did not say, "If you behave, or obey Me, or do so and so, I will do this." He said, "I will do it." It was a unilateral agreement, a one-party contract. Therefore its validity and continuance depend only on the faithfulness of God, not at all on the faithfulness or worth of Abraham or of his descendants. So in Moses' day, when Abraham's descendants had so provoked the wrath of God that He could rightly have utterly destroyed them, Moses pled with Him to remember this promise, and the people were spared (Exod. 32:9-14).

So the nation of Israel, their blessing upon the earth, and their right to the land of Palestine are irrevocably guaranteed by the faithfulness of God himself.

2. **The promise to Moses** (Deut. 4:23-31, 40; chaps. 28–30). Before God brought the children of Israel into their land, He made another promise to them, this time through Moses. The setting was dramatic. Moses had led Israel out of Egypt, given them the law, and endured their waywardness for forty years in the wilderness. Now they were encamped on the east side of the Jordan river, ready to go in and possess the land. At this point there was to be a change of leadership. Moses was to be replaced by Joshua. On the eve of their entry, as his last act of leadership, Moses gathered the people together and delivered a farewell address. This message is our Book of Deuteronomy. Its key phrase is in 1:8: "Go in and possess the land." Its basic message is this promise to Israel, first stated in 4:23-40, often repeated in the book, and solemnly set forth in chapters 28 through 30. Simply stated it is this: Your enjoyment of this land is conditioned upon your obeying the Lord. If you obey, God will bless you in the land. If you disobey, God will punish you in the land, and if need be drive you out of the land. But if you repent, He will bring you back and bless you there.

Look first at Deuteronomy 4:23-31. First there is the warning that if they forget the Lord, they will "soon utterly perish *from off the land*" (vv. 25-26). Then will come a scattering among the nations and captivity (vv. 27-28). Then if they will repent, God will remember His promise to their fathers (vv. 29-31). It is all summarized in verse 40: "Thou shalt keep therefore his statutes, and his commandments . . . that it may go well with thee . . . and that thou mayest prolong thy days *upon the earth* [or land] which the Lord thy God giveth thee, for ever." (See this same sequence in 11:8-28).

Particularly is this truth pressed home in the last chapters of this book. Moses instructed the children of Israel, after they came into the land, to dramatize this new covenant by a formal public ceremony at the twin mountains of Ebal and Gerizim, dividing so that half the tribes stood on one mount and half the tribes on the other. Then they were to recite antiphonally the blessings which God promised to them in the land if they were obedient to the Lord, and the curses which God promised to them if they disobeyed. Going on, Moses foretold that disobedience would drive them out of the land and carry them captive to other nations, there to experience terrible privation, fears, and persecution (Deut. 28:36-37, 49, 63-67). Here the words used go beyond a mere threat of possible punishment and become a prophecy of what would actually happen. Then in 30:1-5 Moses again promised that when these blessings and curses had come and the nation again turned to the Lord, He would bring them back into the land from all the nations where they had been scattered, and bless them in the land.

II. God's Dealing with Israel in History

The history of Israel and God's dealing with them is simply a commentary on these basic Bible truths. Under Joshua they entered and took the land, and God blessed them there. But they forgot God and turned aside to idolatry and sin. God sent foreign nations to oppress them. When their suffering became severe enough they remembered and repented and turned again to the Lord. Then the Lord sent judges who delivered them from their oppressors, and again they were blessed. Soon the cycle started again: sin, oppression, repentance, deliverance. The Book of Judges is a monotonous repetition of this theme over and over again.

Under the kings the same story was repeated, only it became more severe. Finally it became so bad that God sent His people into captivity: the northern kingdom into Assyria, the southern into Babylon for seventy years. True to His word He brought them back and reestablished them in the land. But they still were not ready to be obedient. In fact, when God sent His Messiah to them, they rejected and crucified Him. A few years later God scattered them over the face of the whole earth, where they are to this day, living proof of the faithfulness of God and the truth of God's Word.

III. Is God Through with the Jew?

The answer to this question is so important that it will determine one's whole theological system, and especially his understanding of the subject of prophecy. The question is simply put. Did God end His dealings with Israel as His Chosen People with the destruction of Jerusalem in A.D. 70 and their worldwide dispersion? Or will He again bring them back and bless them in their land? To put it another way, do the prophecies of the Bible which promise future restoration and blessing to Israel under the Messiah refer to the literal nation of Israel, or are they to be applied spiritually to God's present people, the church?

What we have already said regarding the promises of God to Israel ought to make the answer very plain. Remember, God's promise to Abraham and to his seed was *forever* and was *unconditional*. Therefore, nothing that Israel could ever do, not even the rejection of her Messiah, could change that promise. Remember, too, that God prepared us for this present situation by His prophecy through Moses that He *would* so scatter His people and He *would* regather them and bless them. To say God is through with the Jew is to say that God is unfaithful. He promises but He doesn't keep His word.

But let us turn to Romans to see how Paul answers this question. Already in his day it was a problem, even though Israel was still a nation in her own land. For it was obvious that as a nation she had refused her Messiah and was in unbelief respecting the Gospel. The Gospel under Paul's ministry was being preached to Jew and Gentile, and whoever believed was being saved, with no difference between them. How could that situation be reconciled with the Old Testament idea that Israel was God's special people? Why is Israel set aside? Chapters 9 and 10 of Romans deal with the problem from the aspect of divine sovereignty and human responsibility. Then in chapter 11 Paul sets forth two facts which answer the question clearly and decisively.

1. **Israel's setting aside is not complete** (Rom. 11:1-10). To appreciate Paul's words in these verses we must remember that Paul himself was a Jew. The issue we are dealing with here was not a mere theoretical question to him; it was intensely personal. So his answer is quick: Has God cast away His people? God forbid! I'm a Jew! and I know He hasn't cut me off! Then he goes on to explain that there have always been within the national body of Israelites a few who have been faithful, "a remnant according to the election of grace" (v. 5). It was so in Elijah's day. It was true in Paul's day; he was one of these elect. So it is even today. Multi-

tudes of saved Jews are to be found today within the body of Christ, Jews saved by personal faith in the Lord Jesus Christ, today's elect remnant. And God's promises have always been to this elect remnant, not to the bulk of the unbelieving nation (v. 7). So the setting aside of the nation of Israel was only partial.

2. **Israel's setting aside is not final** (Rom. 11:11-32). There is no question, of course, that the nation as a whole had stumbled over the Messiahship of Jesus Christ. Now Paul asks, "Have they stumbled that they should fall?" (v. 11). A stumble is a temporary loss of balance, but a fall is a permanent thing. Israel's present state of unbelief is temporary, and Paul uses this to plead for an active effort on the part of saved Gentiles to evangelize the Jews.

Then in verse 25 he tells us a "mystery," a truth not previously understood but now made clear by divine revelation. This new truth now made known through Paul was "that blindness *in part* [i.e., partial, cf. vv. 1-10] is happened to Israel, *until* [a time-word indicating that this condition is only temporary and will end when] the fulness of the Gentiles be come in." That is, Israel as a nation will remain in unbelief during this age in which the Gospel is going to the whole world. But when the full number of saved Gentiles is reached, this national blindness will end. So he goes on in verse 26, "And so all Israel shall be saved." The nation of Israel will again turn to the Lord in repentance and will again be God's people. Paul even tells us the time: when there comes out of Zion "the Deliverer," the second coming of Christ to deliver His people and establish His kingdom. All this is according to His covenant (v. 27).

So God is not through with the Jew. At the end of this gospel age He will bring them back, restore them to their former place and bless them, according to His promise. Now read verse 29: "For the gifts and calling of God are without repentance." God doesn't change His mind. He keeps His promises.

IV. Prophecies Regarding the Present Situation of the Jew

What does Bible prophecy tell us about the present situation of the Jews? We have already shown that they were to be scattered throughout all the nations of the earth, a prediction so obviously fulfilled as to need no comment. But looking more closely we see remarkable prophecies regarding their condition during this time.

1. **Persecution, hatred, insecurity** (read again Deut. 28:37, 63-68). All this may be summed up in one word, anti-Semitism. Here is a strange phenomenon in human sociological relationships, the unnatural and unexplained animosity of almost all people toward the Jews. From Haman in Persia and Claudius in Rome down through the pages of history the Jews have suffered the indignities of savage hatred. And lest we think this is passing, let us remember with shame what a nominally Christian nation in our day has done, when six million Jews were butchered and burned in Hitler's Germany. Or closer still, let us recall how many fundamentalist preachers have pedaled abroad the old Nazi lie about international Jewry plotting to take control of the world!

Christians should be careful not to allow Satan to trick them into doing his dirty work. Jew-hate is *not* Christian. It is of the devil, as it always has been (read Rev. 13), and it brings the curse of God upon all who participate in it (Gen. 12:3). God's Word prophesied that it would mark the treatment of the Jews during the age of their dispersion, and history amply records the fulfillment of this prophecy.

2. **Preservation.** If anti-Semitism is a sociological puzzle, then the very existence of the Jew is a sociological miracle. By all the rules of cause and effect the Jewish people should long since have perished from the face of the earth. But they are still here. Turn to Hosea 3:4-5 and note the first words of that remarkable prophecy: "The children of Israel *shall abide*." It goes on to explain the unlikely circumstances, "without a king, and without a prince, and without a sacrifice," without political or religious ties to hold them together; yet the Word of God says they shall abide "many days," a long time. For nineteen centuries they have been preserved, without a national home, without a national government, without a national religious system, yet they remain a clearly distinguishable national entity. They have not been assimilated; they have not been destroyed. They abide. So prophecy said, so history records. In fact, the prophet Jeremiah tells us that their future is as certain as the laws of the universe (Jer. 31:35-37).

3. **Prominence.** While I know of no specific Scripture passage which prophesies it, there are at least the typical examples of the past to lead us

to expect that the Jew in his dispersion will frequently be found in places of prominence. Joseph in Egypt, Daniel in Babylon, Mordecai in Persia illustrate the fact from the Scriptures, and history through the years since has witnessed to its continuing truth. Look near the top in almost any realm of human accomplishment and you usually will find a Jew! It is true in science, in mathematics, in art, in music, in literature, in government, in finance, in medicine. It is a remarkable fulfillment of God's promise to Abraham that his seed should be a blessing to the whole world.

V. Prophecies Regarding the Future of Israel

1. **The return of Israel to their land of Palestine.** So many passages speak of this fact that we may take it as one of the assured teachings of prophecy. We have already seen it in the passages used in Deuteronomy (30:3, 5). Isaiah and Jeremiah often combine their messages of coming captivity in Babylon with the assurance that God will bring the people back from captivity, and sometimes in language which goes beyond the return from Babylon, to speak of a final return from all the nations of the earth to a new and holy Jerusalem, never again to be taken away (Isa. 49; 51; 52; Jer. 30; 31; 32; 50:4, 17-20). Ezekiel's well-known "valley of dry bones" (chap. 37) speaks of this restoration as a veritable resurrection from the dead. So marvelous will that event be that it will take the place of the exodus from Egypt in the minds of future generations: "They shall no more say, The Lord liveth, which brought up the children of Israel out of the land of Egypt; but, The Lord liveth, which brought up and which led the seed of the house of Israel out of the north country, and from all countries whither I had driven them; and they shall dwell in their own land" (Jer. 23:7-8).

Sometimes the Bible indicates that this return of the Jews to Palestine will come after the nation has repented and turned to the Lord, and will be accomplished by the Messiah himself after His coming. So in Deuteronomy 30:1-3, "When . . . thou shalt call them to mind among all the nations . . . and shalt return unto the Lord . . . then the Lord . . . will return and gather thee from all the nations."

At other times the Bible indicates that the end time will find the Jews in Jerusalem in a state of unbelief. Ezekiel 36:24-28 says: "I will take you from among the heathen, and gather you out of all countries, and will bring you into your own land. *Then* will I sprinkle clean water upon you, and ye shall be clean. . . . A new heart also will I give you. . . ." Also, the fact that unbelieving Jews in the end time will enter into a covenant with the Antichrist and will endure a time of terrible trouble before their Deliverer comes, with the scene of these events centering in Jerusalem, implies that there will be Jews in the land prior to the Messiah's coming, in sufficient numbers and with national identity so as to be able to "enter a covenant" (Dan. 9:27; 11:41, 45; 12:1).

These two are not in conflict; rather they furnish us with a most remarkable fulfillment of prophecy. We are all familiar with the amazing return of the Jews to Palestine which has been taking place in our own time, and the establishment of the modern nation of Israel in 1948. Perhaps we are growing accustomed to it and the wonder of it is beginning to wear off, but it ought not! It is one of the clearest evidences of the hand of God at work in our day.

Many have wondered, is this the final return of the Jews to their land, the one prophesied in the Bible? The answer must be twofold. No, it is not the final return, for prophecy indicates that that will not come until after Messiah's return, and it will be a return of converted, godly, believing Jews to enter the millennial kingdom. But prophecy also indicates that there must be Jews in the land *prior* to Messiah's coming, unbelieving Jews who will be deceived by Antichrist and will suffer the judgments of God on their nation for its sins. Now it could well be that the present return and the establishment of a modern nation of Israel is the preparation for that final page of their history before Messiah's coming.

Think of it! For nineteen hundred years there would have been no Jews in Palestine to enter a covenant with Antichrist. Now they are there. Truly, they are there in unbelief. Modern Zionism is a political rather than a religious movement. But that is exactly what Bible prophecy would lead us to expect.

2. **The time of Jacob's trouble**. The Bible not only predicts the return of the Jews to Palestine but also tells us what will happen to them there before the arrival of their Messiah. And the picture it paints is not a pleasant one. Jesus himself foretold: "For then shall be great tribulation, such as was not since the beginning of the world to this time, no, nor ever shall be. And except those days should be shortened, there should no flesh

be saved: but for the elect's sake those days shall be shortened. . . . Immediately after the tribulation of those days shall the sun be darkened . . . and then shall appear the sign of the Son of man in heaven: and then shall all the tribes of the earth mourn, and they shall see the Son of man coming in the clouds of heaven with power and great glory" (Matt. 24:21-22, 29-30).

Jeremiah makes it clear that this is particularly a time of trouble for the people of Israel (30:7), and Daniel associates it with the last of the seventy weeks determined upon his people and the covenant with Antichrist (Dan. 12:1; 9:26-27). Many of the prophets describe the coming of the day of the Lord as a time of terrible judgment upon the unbelieving children of Israel for their sins. Read Joel 2, Amos 5:18-20, and Zephaniah 1 for some vivid examples.

The nation of Israel faces some terrible days ahead. And little does she realize that it will not be primarily from her Arab neighbors, but rather it will be the refiner's fire and the fuller's soap by which the Lord will purge her from her iniquity.

3. **The conversion of the nation.** Paul said, "And so all Israel shall be saved" (Rom. 11:26). Zechariah says, "They shall look upon me whom they have pierced, and they shall mourn for him," and that God "will pour upon the house of David, and upon the inhabitants of Jerusalem, the spirit of grace and of supplications" (12:10). He goes on to promise, "I will bring the third part through the fire . . . they shall call on my name, and I will hear them: I will say, it is my people: and they shall say, The Lord is my God" (13:9). Israel rejected her Messiah when He came the first time; but when He comes again, the elect of the nation will receive Him and be saved.

4. **The exaltation of Israel in the millennial kingdom.** The ruler of that glorious kingdom of the millennial age will be the Son of David and He will be sitting on the throne of David. Remember, that is a Jewish throne, in Jerusalem. Although the kingdom will extend over the whole earth and will include all people, yet the Bible makes it clear that Israel is to be in a place of priority. Again, many passages speak of this, but look especially at Isaiah, chapter 60, and note verses 3, 5, 10, 12, and 16.

So brief and so hurried has been this outline of the place of Israel in prophecy that I fear it has not reflected adequately the importance of it. Let us be reminded again that this is the pivotal point in the understanding of all prophetic Scripture. If you are clear at this point, you will not be apt to go very far astray on other points.

SUMMARY

The people of Israel, the Jews, are God's Chosen People and the object of His peculiar blessing.

The land of Palestine has been given to Israel forever, unconditionally.

Their possession and enjoyment of the land depend upon their obedience.

God has temporarily and partially set aside the nation of Israel during the present age of the church, and is offering His message of salvation to all peoples.

When this age is ended, God will again deal with the Jews.

They will return to the land of Palestine, at first in unbelief.

They will there suffer a time of terrible trouble, to destroy the evil and to purge the elect in preparation for the coming of the Messiah.

When Christ comes back the second time, the elect Jews will accept Him as their Messiah and be saved.

Israel will become the central nation in the worldwide kingdom of Christ during the Millennium.

6

~~~~~~

Gentile World Kingdoms
in Prophecy

SUGGESTED BACKGROUND DEVOTIONAL READING	Monday—The King's Dream (Dan. 2:1-13)
	Tuesday—God Answers His Servants (Dan. 2:14-23)
	Wednesday—The Dream's Interpretation (Dan. 2:24-45)
	Thursday—Daniel's Dream (Dan. 7:1-14)
	Friday—Daniel's Dream Interpreted (Dan. 7:15-28)
	Saturday—Vision of the Ram and He Goat (Dan. 8:1-14)
	Sunday—The Vision Explained (Dan. 8:15-27)

INTRODUCTION

The title of this chapter introduces a subject of intense interest. We are all living in a world that is being convulsed by tremendous political movements and events, which are the object of concern, even of worry, on the part of many. As believers who are looking for the coming of Christ and His intervention in world affairs, we are eager to learn all that God has seen fit to tell us about this world's future.

THE AIM

Our aim, then, is to discover and to understand as well as possible what God has said in the prophetic Word about the nations of the world and the political developments of the future. But let it be clearly understood that our aim is not to set up a detailed chart of events by which we can figure out in advance what will happen next. If we approach this subject expecting to learn the fate of Russia, or what will happen to the United States, or the United Nations, or the European Common Market, we are going to be disappointed, even though some preachers like to use such sensational topics to attract attention. Rather, our aim must be spiritual more than intellectual: to encourage on the part of God's people the proper *attitude* toward world history as it happens. This study should produce greater faith and confidence toward God, rather than a greater proficiency in anticipating tomorrow's headlines.

THE DEVELOPMENT

First, we shall trace in broad outline the *course* of Gentile world governments, based on the prophecies of Daniel, and attempt to identify these in history.

Second, we shall take a particular look at the *culmination* of these world powers in the fourth kingdom of Daniel's prophecy, and its place in history and in prophecy.

Third, we shall note the *end* of these world powers and their replacement by God's own world government, considering the manner and time of that end.

Fourth, we shall mention and comment briefly on some other details often associated with this general subject, to see just how much this Word of God actually does have to say about them.

THE EXPOSITION

I. The Course of Gentile World Governments

By far the most important portion of prophetic Scripture to be dealt with in this study is the Book of Daniel, especially chapters 2 and 7, but also including chapters 8, 9, and 11. These are too long for a detailed exposition but certainly should be read carefully.

1. **The setting of these predictions.** These predictions about Gentile world powers come out of the Babylonian Captivity. The nation has lost its kingdom and is under the control of a Gentile world empire. God has determined that His people shall for a period be in subjection. It is at this point that He gives to Daniel the revelation of the course of these Gentile powers. It should be noted that these are Gentile powers related to Israel's national history. There is no attempt to list all Gentile movements or governments, but those that will rule over Israel. In Luke 21:24 our Lord speaks of "the times of the Gentiles," relating them to the subjection of the city of Jerusalem by Gentile conquerors. So the Gentile world powers revealed here to Daniel have to do with the course of empire during "the times of the Gentiles," beginning in Daniel's day with the Babylonian

Captivity and extending to the final restoration of the kingdom to Israel in the days of the Messiah.

2. **The identity of these world empires.** Daniel's prophecy actually gives us two parallel descriptions of this development. In chapter 2 there is the dream of Nebuchadnezzar, in which the succession of kingdoms is seen in the figure of a great image of a man, with the head representing one kingdom, the chest and arms a second, the belly and thighs a third, and the legs and feet a fourth. In chapter 7 we again have a series of four kingdoms, each one represented by a kind of wild beast, after a symbolic pattern which would be natural and easily understood in Daniel's time and place. Since the parallels are so close, we believe that both visions deal with the same four kingdoms.

a. Babylon. The first of these Gentile powers is clearly named for us in Daniel 2:37-38. Daniel tells Nebuchadnezzar that he is the head of gold, representing the Babylonian empire. In chapter 7 the first beast is represented as a lion with eagle's wings. Jeremiah uses both these figures to describe Nebuchadnezzar (Jer. 49:19, 22).

b. Medo-Persia. This second kingdom is represented in chapter 2 by the chest and arms of silver. In chapter 7 it is like a bear, which raises itself up on one side, suggesting a dual kingdom with one part surpassing the other (note that an image of a man has *two* arms). The identification of this second kingdom is not quite so easy, since neither vision names it. But I believe it can be identified positively along with the next one, by reference to chapter 8 (see below).

c. Greece. The third kingdom is represented by the belly and thighs of brass, and by a third beast like a leopard, with four wings of a fowl and four heads. Since this, too, is unnamed, let us look quickly at chapter 8 to see if we can fix the identity of these two.

In the vision of chapter 8 Daniel sees only two beasts, rather than four. It would seem he wants to give additional information about two of these four kingdoms. Can we tell which two? I believe we can. Note that the first of these two was a ram with two horns, one of which was higher and came up last. This would parallel the bear which raised itself up on one side, and the two arms of the image. The second of the beasts in chapter 8 is a he goat with a single horn between its eyes, moving so swiftly that it "touched not the ground." Moreover, when it waxed great the notable horn was broken and there came up in its place four horns. The number four would parallel the four wings and four heads of the leopard, and also in both visions prominence is given to speed of travel ("wings" and "touched not the ground"). So it seems rather clear that the ram of chapter 8 is referring to the same kingdom as the bear of chapter 7, and the goat of chapter 8 is the same as the leopard of chapter 7. Now, in the vision of chapter 8 these kingdoms are clearly named. The ram with the two horns is "the kings of Media and Persia" (v. 20), a dual kingdom at the first with Persia soon taking the place of supremacy. So the second of the great Gentile world powers is Medo-Persia. The goat is named (v. 21) as the king of Grecia, with the single horn representing its first king, Alexander the Great, whose early death brought a division of his kingdom into four parts. So the third great Gentile world power is Greece.

d. Rome. This fourth kingdom becomes the object of special attention in this Book of Daniel, and we shall deal with its identification more particularly in the next section. The fourth kingdom in both visions is described in terms of great strength: "strong as iron: forasmuch as iron breaketh in pieces and subdueth all things" (2:40), "dreadful and terrible, and strong exceedingly; and it had great iron teeth: it devoured and brake in pieces, and stamped the residue with the feet of it" (7:7).

3. **The characteristics of these Gentile world governments.** The Bible has given us two descriptions of these successive kingdoms. The first came to a Gentile king. To his eyes human government looked like an awe-inspiring and glorious thing, a great image of a man—man's estimate of it. The second came to the prophet of God; to his eyes these same kingdoms appeared as a series of dreadful and terrible wild beasts, ravenous and beastly—God's estimate of them.

Note also that there is a decline in nobility but an increase in strength and ferocity in these representations. The image had its head of gold; the next part was of silver, then brass, then iron. The series of beasts begins with the lion, king of beasts, then goes on with a bear, a leopard, and a nondescript beast, dreadful and terrible, which devoured, broke in pieces, and stamped the residue with its feet. These changes seem to reflect the deterioration in nobility from the absolute sovereignty of Nebuchadnezzar to a sovereignty limited by "the laws of the Medes and the Persians," and on to the Roman Empire whose rulers were subject to a Senate. The corresponding increase in strength is seen in the fact that Rome was in history the strongest and largest of them all. The introduction of the clay into the feet and toes of the image is explained as a sudden loss of strength in the final stages of the fourth kingdom by "mingling with the seed of men," perhaps a reference to democracy or communism.

II. The Culmination of Gentile World Government

Both visions of the four Gentile kingdoms place special attention on the fourth. Daniel himself asked for and received an explanation of this one particularly (7:19-28). It is the last of the four, and is most significant. It is very important, therefore, to learn the identity of this one and the meaning of the details given regarding it.

1. **The importance of the fourth kingdom.** Both visions emphasize its strength and its terribleness. The beasts chosen to describe the other three kingdoms are familiar ones: lion, bear, leopard. But this one is not likened to any known beast. Three times we are told it was diverse (different) from all the others. Perhaps we may conceive of it as a composite, made up of elements of all the others. At least in the Book of Revelation a similar beast is described as "like unto a leopard, and his feet were as the feet of a bear, and his mouth as the mouth of a lion." This beast also had ten horns and represents a king of a kingdom closely related to this fourth kingdom.

Daniel gives special emphasis to the horns and what takes place among them. The beast at first has ten horns; then another little horn comes up and plucks out three horns, and in it appear eyes and a mouth speaking great things. The angel explains that "out of this kingdom are ten kings that shall arise" (7:24). Then after them another king will arise, subdue three of his predecessors, speak great blasphemies against the true God, persecute the saints of God, and attempt to alter the customs and laws. We are told he will continue "until a time [one year] and times [two years] and the dividing of time [one-half year]," or three and one-half years (7:25).

This personage introduced as the little horn arising on the head of the fourth beast will be our next special study, the Antichrist. He becomes the special theme of the rest of Daniel's prophecy. In chapter 8 the ram and goat vision traces the history of the second and third kingdom from

Daniel's own day down to the appearance of a historic person known to us by the name of Antiochus Epiphanes, whose persecution of the Jews makes him a type of that future Antichrist. In chapter 9 he appears as the prince that will come in the seventieth week of Israel's future to make a covenant with them and later to break it. In chapters 10 through 12, or more particularly chapter 11, again the history is traced down to the same Antiochus, then goes beyond him to Antichrist.

For our present purpose it should be noted that this little horn, which represents the Antichrist, arises out of and becomes the dominant power in the fourth great world empire.

This fourth Gentile world power, then, is the last. Daniel's prophecies are very specific on this point. The great image of Nebuchadnezzar comes to a sudden and violent end when "a stone cut out without hands" smote the image *on the feet* and broke it to pieces, and the stone "became a great mountain, and filled the whole earth" (2:34-35). This is explained: "In the days of kings [plural, probably referring to the toes, v. 42] shall the God of heaven set up a kingdom, which shall never be destroyed . . . it shall break in pieces and consume all these kingdoms, and it shall stand for ever" (2:44). Similarly the beast vision of chapter 7 climaxes at the throne of the Ancient of Days, when the fourth beast is slain; one like unto the Son of Man comes in the clouds of heaven, and a kingdom is given to him, a kingdom that will never be destroyed (7:9, 11, 13, 14).

So in Daniel's prophecy we have seen a prophetic preview of the course of Gentile world powers from his own day until the time when God would intervene to set up His own kingdom. The Gentile kingdoms would be four: Babylon, Medo-Persia, Greece, and a fourth not named but especially important because of its violence and persecution of God's people in the days of a terrible king that would arise out of it. Then, in the midst of the ungodly defiance of this fourth kingdom God would step in miraculously to destroy and bring to an end the whole period of Gentile power and set up His own kingdom under the Messiah, to last forever.

2. **The identification of this fourth kingdom.** Now let us look at this fourth kingdom from our vantage point and seek to identify it. Historically, it must be Rome. Rome replaced and succeeded Greece just as Greece had replaced Persia, and Persia succeeded Babylon. Also, in Daniel 9:26 we are told that Messiah's cutting off and the destruction of the city of

Jerusalem would be brought about by the "people of the prince that shall come." That prince is the little horn of this fourth kingdom, so it was the people of this fourth kingdom that cut off Messiah and destroyed Jerusalem. From the New Testament we know these people to be Romans.

3. **The problem with this identification.** When we determine that Rome is the fourth and last Gentile world power, we run into problems. Why are there no more? Why does the inspired writer stop here? For the Roman Empire has passed off the scene. There have been many Gentile powers since, and there are many at the present time. How, then, can Rome be last?

In answer, let it be recalled what we said first. These are Gentile powers which ruled over God's Chosen People, Israel, in their land. Rome *was* the last Gentile power that ruled over the nation of Israel as a nation. During the Roman period Israel ceased to be a nation.

But even more pertinent is the recognition that a great gap of time is involved in the interpretation of Daniel. This is most clearly seen in a study of chapter 9, the "seventy weeks" prophecy. Daniel 9:24 tells us that "seventy weeks [of years] are determined upon thy people and upon thy holy city." The rest of that verse identifies the accomplishments with which this time-period will end: "To finish the transgression, and to make an end of sins, and to make reconciliation for iniquity, and to bring in everlasting righteousness, and to seal up the vision and prophecy, and to anoint the most Holy [or the most holy place]." These terms in their Jewish context can refer only to the spiritual salvation of Israel and the setting up of the messianic kingdom. Now these seventy sevens are divided into three parts. The first seven of sevens (forty-nine years) began with the decrees of Artaxerxes in 445 B.C. to restore and to rebuild the city of Jerusalem, and seems to cover the period of reconstruction. The second part is sixty-two weeks; it follows the first seven without a break and brings us to the time of the Messiah. Then before the third part of the time sequence, the seventieth week, is mentioned, there is an interruption (v. 26). Messiah will be cut off, and the city and the temple of Jerusalem will be destroyed and apparently rebuilt, for the description of the last week shows the temple standing and functioning. Then after an interruption of undetermined length the sequence is resumed, with a Roman prince making a covenant with many of the Jews for one week, the seventieth and last week of the prophetic period.

This interruption or gap in the time-sequence is explained when we come to the New Testament. Messiah did come during the Roman kingdom, but His people rejected Him and turned Him over to the Romans to crucify Him. As a result, the kingdom was postponed until He should come back a second time, this time in power to set it up by force. The years between the first and second coming of Christ, then, are a gap in history not seen by Daniel. The Jews, after their rejection of their Messiah, were set aside for a time as God's nation. Their city was destroyed, their national entity lost. As one Bible teacher has described it, the clock of God's dealings with Israel stopped. Some day He will start it again, and it will run for another seven years. So Daniel's picture of Gentile world rulers simply omits all the years since Christ's first coming.

This isn't all the matter, however. Daniel does describe the Gentile world power during those last seven years. In fact, he emphasizes especially that period of Gentile rule, under the visions of the little horn and the typology of Antiochus Epiphanes. And he identifies this endtime ruler as the fourth kingdom. Therefore the Gentile world power when Christ comes the second time will be Rome. It can't be any new power, because that would be a fifth, and there are to be only four. And it is this fourth kingdom which is destroyed by the stone cut out without hands, or by the coming of Messiah and the setting up of God's kingdom. So if Rome was the world power when Christ came the first time, and Rome is to be the world power when He returns, then the logical conclusion is that the Roman Empire will be revived in the last days.

As a matter of fact, Rome was never replaced by a fifth world power. The Roman Empire broke in pieces and disintegrated, but no new world power destroyed it or took its place. Its memory, even its titles and crowns, have been perpetuated, first in the assumptions of the Holy Roman Empire, and more recently in the modern European countries. Roman law is still the basis of Western civilization. So in a sense, the Roman world empire still continues. Of course, its revival in the end time will be as an actual world power.

III. The End of Gentile World Governments

We have already anticipated this point in showing that the fourth kingdom was to be the *last*. Gentile world government will come to a violent and catastrophic end with the coming of Messiah.

Many have tried to solve the problem of why Rome is the last Gentile power named by interpreting the setting up of this kingdom of God as the victory of the church, or of the Gospel. They say this is Christ's spiritual kingdom in the hearts of men. But aside from the fact that such a spiritual kingdom is not taught elsewhere in the Scriptures, it doesn't even solve the problem here. For this kingdom which Messiah sets up in these passages in Daniel actually destroys, brings to an end, and replaces the Roman Empire, whereas this so-called spiritual kingdom admittedly does not either destroy or replace the worldly powers, but is conceived as existing alongside of them. Also, instead of Christ destroying the Roman power when He came, it crucified Him. This explanation of the Daniel passage is completely wrong. It doesn't explain anything, and it introduces a wholly unscriptural idea.

The consistent teaching of Scripture everywhere is that human kingdoms will some day come to a sudden and violent end, when God again intervenes in human affairs with the second coming of Christ to set up His perfect and final kingdom.

IV. Other Details

Many questions arise when we look at the teaching of the prophetic Scriptures regarding the nations of the world. We often wish we could know more of the details, or discover answers to our specific questions. This is not always possible. But instead of being disappointed that the Bible does not tell more, we must rather marvel and thank God that it has told so much. Does it have anything more to say about the Gentile nations?

1. **Other world powers of the end time.** Prophecy does mention certain other powers in connection with the fourth kingdom and the Antichrist of the end time. In Daniel 11:40-45 there is mentioned a king of the north and a king of the south. Also it speaks of tidings out of the east and of the north, which seems to refer to other political powers of the end time. Can these be identified?

It must be kept in mind that the Antichrist rises to power gradually, and his absolute, worldwide power seems to come only in the last half of the seventieth week of Daniel. Therefore, the other forces in conflict with him in Daniel 11:40-45 probably belong to the first half of the week. The king of the north, if this does not refer to Antichrist himself, would represent a power north of Palestine, therefore Syria, Lebanon, Turkey, or Russia. The king of the south would represent Egypt and perhaps the African nations behind her. The east might refer to Japan or China or India. These are interesting speculations, but the Bible does not give any absolute proof or any details, and it is out of place for us to be dogmatic.

2. **The invasion of Gog** (Ezek. 38–39). Here is a prophetic passage dealing with a Gentile power of the end time where the Bible does tell us much. It predicts an invasion of Palestine by a northern power comprised of many nations, including Gog, Persia, Ethiopia, Libya, Gomer, and Togarmah. Who are these? There has been much speculation on the basis of similarity of sounds and supposed etymologies, identifying Gog with Russia, Gomer with Germany, Togarmah with Turkey, and so forth. As a result there has been much said about a Russian invasion of Palestine. Sober Bible study, however, shows that these names refer to various ancient people living north of Palestine in the central and eastern parts of Turkey and in Armenia and around the Black Sea. But since this northern invasion belongs to the end time, and right now at least the chief power north of Palestine is Soviet Russia, it is not improbable that this prophecy may refer to such.

At the time of this invasion Israel is dwelling in the land in peace and security, enjoying considerable wealth, for the purpose of the invasion is for spoil. This would indicate that the invasion occurs *before* the Jews come under the terrible persecution of the Antichrist, therefore before the middle of the last week. It therefore cannot be a reference to Armageddon, which comes at the end of the last week. If we identify Gog as the king of the north in Daniel 11:40, then this northern invasion might be placed at the middle of the seventieth week. If we do not make this identification, then this northern invasion could occur anytime before the middle of the seventieth week, possibly even before its beginning.

3. **Is the United States in prophecy?** This is always an exciting question, but I am convinced that the answer is not so exciting. Of course, there are general passages which speak of the whole earth, and all that dwell on the

face of the earth, which would include the United States along with the rest. But so far as I have been able to discover, there is no clear reference in the Bible to any nation that can be identified as the United States.

SUMMARY

Four great Gentile world powers are identified in the Bible from Daniel's time to the establishment of God's messianic kingdom.

The fourth of these was Rome, the world empire in existence at the coming of the Messiah the first time.

There have been none since, and there will be none, until Christ comes again.

At the time of Christ's second coming the Roman Empire will again be in power, revived for its role in the end-time events.

This final Roman world power will be headed up by a terrible person whom we call Antichrist.

When Christ comes back in power and glory to set up His kingdom, He will destroy and bring to an end forever the Gentile world powers.

Some interesting speculations about other details should be carefully guarded lest we be too dogmatic.

God has told us these things in order that we might not be troubled at the events which come to pass.

7

The Antichrist and the Great Tribulation

SUGGESTED **BACKGROUND** **DEVOTIONAL** **READING**	Monday—Great Tribulation (Matt. 24:15-30) Tuesday—Antichrist, Man of Sin (II Thess. 2:1-10) Wednesday—Antichrist Will Come (I John 2:18-25) Thursday—The Prince That Will Come (Dan. 9:24-27) Friday—He Will Magnify Himself (Dan. 11:36—12:1) Saturday—All the World Will Wonder (Rev. 13:1-9) Sunday—The End of Antichrist (Rev. 19:11-21)

INTRODUCTION

Our attention has been called to a terrible personage related to the last great Gentile world government. Now we want to look more closely at this person and see what Bible prophecy has to say about him and his times. We might call this study "The Coming World Dictator and His Superstate," or "The Last Seven Years of Human History."

THE AIM

As we pursue this study it ought to accomplish at least three aims for us. It should (1) open our eyes to the terrible potential for evil which lies in the human heart and in human society, (2) warn us of the awful consequences of sin and the judgment that God is going to bring on it in His own time, and (3) persuade men not to let the day of salvation go by unheeded. As we examine the following Scriptures, keep constantly in mind that this is what is ahead for all who do not accept Christ as Saviour.

THE DEVELOPMENT

First, we shall look at the person of Antichrist, his character, his origin, and his identity.

Second, we shall trace the career of Antichrist, how he rises to power, the stage of his career, and the description of his world government.

Third, we shall describe the times of Antichrist, seeking to make clear what conditions will be like in his day, how his rule will affect believers and unbelievers, and what God will be doing during those tremendous times. What will life on earth be like during the last seven years of human history?

THE EXPOSITION

I. The Person of Antichrist

1. **References to him.** The Antichrist is an actual historical person who will come into world prominence in the end time. This person is called by various names and titles in the Bible. Daniel speaks of his emergence out of the last great world empire as the prominent political leader of the end time, calling him in his symbolic language "a little horn" (7:8), and in his explanation "another king" (7:24), "the prince that shall come" (9:26), "the king" who does according to his will (11:36), and perhaps the "king of fierce countenance" (8:23). Paul calls him "that man of sin" and "that Wicked [One]" (II Thess. 2:3, 8). Apostle John is the one who uses the name by which he has come to be known best, the Antichrist (I John 2:18). Also, in his Book of Revelation he calls him "the beast" (13:1 and through the rest of the book). While these are the chief passages which deal with this person, he is probably to be seen in many others, for example in Genesis 3:15 as the seed of the serpent, and in Psalm 110:6 (ASV) as the head over many nations.

2. **His character.** From these passages we gather a description of the character of this person. He has a most remarkable personality. He is different from the ordinary man and stands out conspicuously even among his fellow kings (Dan. 7:20, 24). He is highly intelligent ("eyes," Dan. 7:8), an unusually gifted, powerful speaker (Dan. 7:8, 20, 25), a philosopher of note (Dan. 8:23), a crafty politician (Dan. 8:25), a great military genius (Rev. 13:4, 7). In religion he will be a materialistic pantheist, honoring only himself as the god of military force (Dan. 11:36-39). Because of his remarkable career, and perhaps because of his personality, "all the world wondered after the beast" (Rev. 13:3). Yet the Book of Revelation aptly describes him in the term it uses; he is a "beast."

Especially is one characteristic of his person emphasized in the Scriptures, his sin. Paul calls him the "man of sin," and "that Wicked [One]" (II Thess. 2:3, 8). Daniel and the Revelation emphasize his blasphemous utterances against God (Dan. 7:25; 11:36; Rev. 13:6) and his setting himself up over all gods, even demanding worship as a god. He will be the very incarnation of sin, pride, rebellion, and ambition.

3. **His origin.** Where does this person come from? The Bible leaves no doubt in this respect.

a. Politically, he rises "out of the sea" (Rev. 13:1). In symbolic terms the sea speaks of the turmoil and restlessness and political uncertainty of all the nations. This would agree with other passages which speak of the end time as a time of "wars and rumours of wars," "distress of nations, with perplexity; the sea and the waves roaring; men's hearts failing them for fear" (Luke 21:25-26). This political unrest may assist the Antichrist in his rise to power.

b. Nationally, he will be a Roman (Dan. 9:26). Daniel pictures him as arising out of the fourth world empire, the Roman. And it was his people who crucified Christ and destroyed the city of Jerusalem. He will be the future head of the revived Roman Empire.

c. Racially, many have concluded that he will be a Jew. This is based on the statement that he will not regard "the God of his fathers" (Dan. 11:37), a verse, however, which could just as well read, "the gods of his ancestors." Also, it is argued that the Jews would not enter into a covenant with him or accept him as their Messiah if he were not a Jew. But so far as the present writer has been able to discover, there is no Biblical warrant for the idea that the Jews' covenant with the Roman prince will be based on their acceptance of him as Messiah. Such a notion seems to be based on John 5:43, although there is nothing in that passage to suggest it. Therefore, the idea that the Antichrist will be a Jew must be regarded as very improbable.

d. Spiritually, he rises "out of the bottomless pit [the abyss]" (Rev. 11:7). This abyss (Rev. 9:1) is the place where the evil spirits or demons are kept locked up, and this may mean that the Antichrist will be a demon incarnate, or a man possessed with a demon. Certainly he will be Satan's man, and Satan will be the power behind his throne.

e. Providentially, he will be from God, in the sense that his going forth will be in God's time and under God's permissive direction to accomplish God's predetermined purpose (II Thess. 2:11; Rev. 6:1-2).

4. **His identity.** Other than these general statements the identity of Antichrist is unknown and must remain so until after the Rapture of the church. Second Thessalonians 2:7-8 makes it absolutely clear that he will not be revealed until after the restrainer is taken away, that is, after the Rapture of the church. So speculation as to whether such-and-such a person prominent in the news is Antichrist is not only useless, it is sinful. After that time the people on earth who are willing to believe God's Word will recognize him by his number, 666 (Rev. 13:18). Again, attempts to decipher his cryptic number are useless until the time comes.

II. The Career of Antichrist

1. **His rise to power.** His career will be launched with an inconspicuous beginning. Daniel says that in the time when the fourth world empire is being ruled by ten kings, represented by the ten horns, "there came up among them another little horn" (7:8), "after them" (7:24). However, this small beginning very quickly gives way to a spectacular rise to prominence: "Before whom there were three of the first horns plucked up by the roots" (7:8). The language which follows makes it clear that the Antichrist quickly becomes the real head of the ten-power confederacy, which will be the form of this revived Roman Empire (Rev. 17:12-13). As the prince of the Roman people he enters into a seven-year covenant, or treaty, with the Jewish nation in Palestine.

It seems clear, however, that the Antichrist is not unopposed in his bid for world power, at least during the first part of his career. There are indications of the opposition in Daniel 11:40, where the king of the south (Egypt and perhaps Africa) pushes at him. In the rest of this verse there is a difference of opinion as to the proper rendering, whether the king of the north is Antichrist, or whether he may be another hostile power coming against Antichrist, perhaps Gog of Ezekiel 38-39. If the latter interpretation is accepted, then verses 40-45 are referring not to Antichrist, but to the king of the north. At any rate, in verse 44 two new hostile quarters are mentioned, tidings out of the east (Japan or China or India or Persia; we cannot be dogmatic) and out of the north (Rome or Europe or Russia or Turkey; again we cannot be sure). So it seems clear that Antichrist will face a host of enemies in his rise to power but ultimately will be victorious over them all.

Here Revelation 13:3 and 14 may have an interesting connection. This passage tells us that the beast (Antichrist) will receive a deadly wound which will be healed, causing all the world to wonder after him. In the original of the passage it seems clear that he actually is killed in battle and miraculously brought back to life. No wonder they will wonder after him!

Several factors may help to account for such a remarkable rise to power in so short a time. The Bible indicates that the world will be in a state of chaos and political confusion from its wars and rumors of wars. Conditions will be right for the rise of a strong man and for his acceptance by the desperate people. Compare the rise to power of Hitler out of the confusion of World War I. Or, suppose right now a strong man should appear in the United Nations who would be dramatically successful in solving the various crises threatening world peace. There are many who would be ready to support such a one for whatever position to which he might aspire. Other factors that help account for Antichrist's rapid rise to power are his own personal abilities, the support of the Jews, the support of apostate religion (the ecumenical church of the end time, Rev. 17:1-7), and the miraculous workings of Satan in his behalf (II Thess. 2:9; Rev. 13:4, 11-13). Also, it must be remembered that God in His providence inflicts judicial blindness, "strong delusion," on the unbelievers of that day so that they will believe the "lie" of Antichrist (II Thess. 2:11).

2. **His superstate.** The world government of Antichrist is described with considerable detail in the Scriptures. It will be a political dictatorship based on military power (Rev. 13:7, 10). Although he begins as one among ten kings of the revived Roman Empire, yet these ten all turn over their power to him and he rules with absolute authority (Rev. 17:12-13, 17). It will be an economic dictatorship (Rev. 13:16-17), so powerful that it will be illegal for anyone in the whole world to buy or sell without identifying himself with Antichrist and receiving the mark of the Beast. It will be a religious dictatorship as well (Rev. 13:15), demanding that the worship of all men be addressed to the Beast himself and to his image. A false prophet from Satan will use miracles and wonders to persuade and enforce this worship of Satan's Messiah, thus bringing into existence a satanic trinity in those terrible last days, with Satan taking the place of God the Father,

Antichrist taking the place of Christ, the Son of God, and the false prophet taking the place of the Holy Spirit (Rev. 13:4, 11-12).

When Antichrist sets himself up as God and demands worship, it is obvious that he no longer is going to recognize or support the other religious elements of that time. There are two of these, and the Bible has clearly indicated the relations of Antichrist to both of them. The first is the Jews. At the very beginning of his career he enters a covenant, or an agreement, with the Jews for seven years, the last of Daniel's seventy weeks. This agreement, from its context, seems to deal with the Jews' possession of the land of Palestine or the city of Jerusalem. Perhaps in return for their support he agrees to make available to them the site of the temple (which is now in Arab hands and occupied by a Moslem mosque) for the building of their new temple—what wouldn't Israel do for anyone who could make an offer like that! But when he comes to the middle of this seven-year covenant, he suddenly turns against the Jews, breaks his covenant, stops the sacrifices in the rebuilt temple, and sets up the abomination of desolation in the holy place, demanding that the Jews worship him as God.

The other religious body of that time also bears a special relationship to the Antichrist. In Revelation 17 there is presented a woman arrayed in purple and scarlet, decked with gold and precious stones and pearls. She is called "the great whore," or harlot, who sits on many waters and has committed fornication with the kings of the earth, "that great city, which reigneth over the kings of the earth." This strange figure seems to represent false religion, or apostate Christianity, in its unholy alliance with the political world and its persecution of the true believers. Since it is *one* figure, it would appear that the modern drive for ecumenicity will have succeeded by that time, and the similarities between this woman and the Roman Catholic religion would suggest that this ecumenical movement has actually meant that the "separated brethren" have come home to Rome! Now the point to note here is that this woman at first rides upon the Beast (vv. 3, 7). The Antichrist at first supports the apostate religious system of the day, just as he does the Jewish religion. But he does so only so long as it suits his convenience. In verses 15-17 he turns on the woman as he did on the Jews, and his associates destroy her. Thus even false and apostate religion will succumb to the ambitions of this anti-god world power who demands that he alone be worshiped as God.

So the world will finally get its one-world, its world state, its world government. The tendency of empire has always been toward world domination. Alexander, we are told, wept on the shores of the Indus River because there were no more kingdoms to conquer. Charlemagne, Charles V, Napoleon, Kaiser Wilhelm, Hitler, Communist Russia, all dreamed of ruling the world. The League of Nations and our present United Nations have been attempts to set up a world-government system. Today, even in America, there are strange voices advocating the surrender of national sovereignty in the interest of a united world power. Logically, this seems to be the next step. Nationalism has produced wars and tensions. World peace, it is argued, depends on the cooperation of nations in a one-world organization.

Well, prophecy indicates that this one-world government will come some day in the superstate of the superman, Antichrist. It is the only form of human government man has not yet tried. It, too, will be tried, and will fail, as final proof of man's inability to govern himself. Then will Messiah come to set up God's kingdom over men, a perfect kingdom that will demonstrate what a wonderful world this world can be when it is run right!

III. The Times of Antichrist

What will things be like on the earth under the rule of Antichrist? The Bible describes them with great detail and vividness in Revelation 4–19. We need to distinguish three periods of his rule.

1. **During the first part of his reign.** The rise of Antichrist to power takes place during the first half of Daniel's seventieth week, the three and one-half years immediately following the Rapture of the church. World conditions at that time are described for us in Revelation 6–7 under the figure of the breaking of the seals, as Christ receives the title deed to the control of the earth and exercises His authority by opening its seals. First, there go forth in quick succession four horsemen, symbolizing (1) the rise of Antichrist (the white horse and its rider), (2) worldwide wars (the red horse), (3) famine and scarcity (the black horse), and (4) death or pestilence (the pale horse). By these a fourth of all the people on earth will be killed. The opening of the fifth seal introduces a scene in heaven in

which the souls of martyred believers are under the altar, waiting for their number to be completed. This is a picture of religious persecution and calls forth a vision in Revelation 7:9-17 of an unnumbered multitude of such martyred saints in heaven, people saved out of the tribulation period who pay with their lives for their faith in Christ.

These early judgments of the period of Antichrist appear thus to be providential judgments which God brings to pass by the natural working out of the laws of cause and effect. Sin is reaping its whirlwind, as it sweeps on without restraint. Its consequences are terrible indeed.

2. **During the last half of his reign, when his power is supreme.** This particularly seems to be the period of time when Jesus called "the tribulation, the great one" (Matt. 24:21-22). For the Jews it will be the "time of Jacob's trouble," when God's Chosen People will be put through the purging fires of God's judgment to burn out and destroy the dross and to purify His elect. The prophets seem to exhaust human language in trying to describe the terrors of that time. For those who during that awful period turn to God in faith, it will be a continuation of the persecutions begun under the fifth seal, until the number of martyrs will defy counting; most if not all the converts of that era will die for their faith. On the rest of the world, the godless and unbelieving dwellers on the earth who have aligned themselves with Antichrist and received his mark, there will be a terrifying succession of unimaginable judgments from the wrath of God.

Now these judgments go beyond the providential use of natural consequences. God will bring to pass a series of miraculous acts of judgment for the purpose of destroying sin and punishing sinners and wresting the control of this old world out of the hands of its present world rulers, to prepare it for the coming of the rightful ruler and the setting up of a kingdom of righteousness. These judgments remind us often of the plagues God brought on Egypt in the time of Moses, but they are more terrible and they involve the entire world. The sounding of the seven trumpets and the pouring out of the last seven vials of God's wrath upon the world describe conditions which our minds find difficult to conceive. If they are literal, that is bad enough. If they are symbols, they are symbols of a reality more terrible even than the literal pictures used to describe them. They leave men crawling into the holes and caves of the earth and calling on the rocks to fall on them and to hide them from the wrath of God being poured out upon them in all its fury.

3. **The Bible also portrays the final days of that terrible period and the end of Antichrist's reign.** We are told of a great army which Antichrist gathers against Jerusalem and the remnant of God's people still preserved there, of the gathering of this army in a place called Armageddon (Rev. 16:14, 16), and of its destruction there from "the sword that proceedeth out of the mouth" of the King of kings and Lord of lords, the Lord Jesus Christ as He comes from heaven in power and glory to set up His kingdom. Here we learn the fate of the Antichrist. He is captured and thrown alive into the lake of fire, the hell of God's eternal judgment (Rev. 19:20). And he is still there a thousand years later, when he is joined by the devil himself (Rev. 20:10).

Thus ends the final world dictator and his superstate. The stone cut out of the mountain without hands has fallen upon the feet of the image, and the whole image is ground into the chaff of the threshing floor to be carried away with the wind. Next that stone will become a great mountain and fill the whole earth, and the God of heaven will set up a kingdom which will never be destroyed.

SUMMARY

Human history will someday reach its climax in a terrible person who will be the culmination of sin and godlessness. He will be the absolute head of the final Gentile world power, and revived Roman Empire, and the last great human leader of history. He will be Satan's Messiah for the human race.

Antichrist will make a covenant with the Jewish nation for seven years. In the midst of that time he will turn against the Jews, stop their sacrifices, and set himself up as God, demanding worship from them. He will also destroy apostate Christendom.

His times will be times of great tribulation and trouble for the Jews, for the ones who accept Christ and are saved during those days, and for all the people on the earth. This will be the day of wrath, the day of vengeance of our God, such as never was before and never will be again.

Antichrist will come to his end when Christ comes and destroys him with the brightness of His coming, placing him eternally in the lake of fire.

8

The Church in Prophecy

INTRODUCTION

We have attempted to trace the prophetic picture of Israel and of the Gentile nations in prophetic Scripture. One other body of people is yet to be considered—the church. This body, which began on the Day of Pentecost and will end its earthly sojourn in the Rapture when Christ comes back for His own, is composed of all true believers in the Lord Jesus Christ, all who by faith have experienced personal salvation. The identity of this "mystical" or "invisible" church, however, is known only to God. So far as our knowledge of it is concerned, it is represented by the "visible" church, the nominal or professing church, the local congregation or congregations. It is in this sense that we use the word when we look at the church in prophecy. What does the Bible teach us to expect will happen in the church as this age progresses?

THE AIM

This chapter should accomplish at least two aims. (1) It should encourage us to see that in spite of seeming failures, God's will is being worked out and will ultimately prevail. And (2) it should challenge us to make sure that we, and the church we are a part of, are faithful to our Lord and fulfilling His will for us.

THE DEVELOPMENT

Basically, there are three approaches which Scripture makes to this problem.

First, there is the series of "parables of the kingdom" in Matthew 13. We shall attempt to explain the basic application of these parables to the church age.

Second, there are passages which tell the purpose and program of God for the church in our age. These will help us to see how God's plan is working out through the church.

Third, there are several passages which speak of the course of this age and describe "the last days." We shall select one of these and relate it to our present subject.

Fourth, there is a remarkable "prophetic history" of the church age to be seen in the series of letters to the seven churches of Asia in Revelation 2 and 3. We shall trace this prophetic development briefly, and shall look more particularly at the last one.

THE EXPOSITION

I. The Kingdom Parables of Matthew 13

1. **The peculiar nature and significance of these parables.** As we begin reading the thirteenth chapter of Matthew, we are immediately made aware of a change of tone or of emphasis. The disciples themselves noticed it. After Jesus had finished the parable of the sower, they came to Him and asked, "Why are you speaking to them in parables?" They were not asking why He used parables. The reason for parables or illustrations is self-evident in the clearer understanding they give. Besides, this was not the beginning of Christ's use of parables (cf. Matt. 7:3-5, 24-27; 11:16-17; Luke 5:36-39; 6:39; 7:40-47, all earlier in time than Matt. 13). When they asked "Why?" they showed that there was something different about these parables. These parables puzzled them. They came and requested, "Explain this parable to us." Most stories or illustrations don't need explaining; rather, they explain other things. But these did need explanation. That was the difference.

In Jesus' explanation He used a quotation from the Old Testament which recurs several times in the rest of the New Testament, always at a significant time of crisis. Taken from Isaiah, it speaks of eyes that won't see, ears that won't hear, and a judicial act of God in rendering such incapable of seeing and hearing. No eye is so blind as one that *will* not see.

From one who closes his eyes because he does not want to see, God takes away the ability to see. All this is said in the context of chapter 12, where we see the opposition of the unbelieving Jews rising to a climax of hate and rejection, until they are accusing the Son of God of being in league with the devil. The awfulness of their refusal to believe is reflected there by the most solemn pronouncement ever to fall from Jesus' lips, His statement regarding an unpardonable sin. Now, speaking in the presence of these willful unbelievers, He speaks in parables, strange parables which need to be explained before they can perform their function of teaching and illustrating truths. They are a judgment on unbelief: "It is given unto you to know the mysteries of the kingdom of heaven, but to them it is not given" (13:11).

2. **The mysteries of the kingdom.** This is the term Jesus used to express what He was talking about in these parables. These parables teach us about the mysteries of the kingdom of heaven.

We are familiar with the term "kingdom of heaven," but it is so widely misused these days that we need to explain briefly. When John the Baptist began his ministry, his message was "Repent ye: for the kingdom of heaven is at hand" (Matt. 3:2). With the same theme Jesus himself began His ministry (Matt. 4:17). No explanation is offered; a simple announcement is made. Evidently it was understood, for no one raised the question: What do you mean? You see, this term was one which was familiar to the people of His day. The prophets of the Old Testament had been talking for centuries of the coming of a glorious kingdom which the God of heaven would set up. When the people heard the announcement that the kingdom of heaven, or the kingdom of God, was at hand, they understood. To them it meant the wonderful kingdom of the Messiah. Evidently Jesus intended them to understand it so, for He never tried to correct their "false notion" or to define His terms differently. Now when He speaks of the mysteries of the kingdom, He must be understood to be talking about that same kingdom, the reign of God over this earth by the Messiah.

The word "mystery" is not so commonly understood. To us the English word might suggest something mysterious or deep or hard to be understood. And some have thought that these parables deal with the deeper, hidden, spiritual aspects of the kingdom. But this is not the primary meaning of the word in the original; in fact, it is doubtful whether it ever carries this meaning in the Bible. Rather, the word refers to a truth known only through revelation. It is used of a truth which previously was not known, but now has been told. When this meaning is applied to the present passage, the expression "the mysteries of the kingdom of heaven" means "hitherto unrevealed aspects of the kingdom of God."

The Old Testament told much about that coming kingdom. But now, in view of the unbelief and rejection and spiritual blindness of Israel, Jesus is going to reveal to His disciples some new truths about that kingdom, never mentioned in the Old Testament prophecies. These new truths have reference to the changes in the prospects of the kingdom brought about by the Jews' rejection. Jesus soon makes it plain that the kingdom will be postponed until His second advent (Luke 19:11-12) and that in the meantime He will inaugurate a new body of believers called the church (Matt. 16:16-18). This is a new thing, wholly unseen and unrevealed in the Old Testament. So the term Jesus uses, "the mysteries," the previously unrevealed part of the kingdom of heaven, refers to the fortunes of God's kingdom during the period of postponement, the church age.

Some may object to this applying of kingdom truth to the church, on the ground that the church and the kingdom are not the same. Of course they are not the same. We insist that the Old Testament kingdom prophecies do *not* refer to the church, but to the future, literal establishment of God's kingdom on earth. But it is also clear that the church is related to that future kingdom. When the kingdom does come, the church, the bride of Christ, is to live and reign with Him over that kingdom (Rev. 20:6). Even now, when a person is saved he is translated out of the kingdom of darkness into the kingdom of God's dear Son (Col. 1:13). So the church, although distinct from the kingdom, does have a place in it. It is, in fact, the previously unrevealed aspect of the kingdom.

3. **The prophetic teaching of the kingdom parables.** An exposition of all these seven parables is unnecessary for our present purpose. We want only briefly to see what they teach us about the course of this interim age in which we are now living.

The first parable, that of the sower, is explained by Christ himself. It tells us that during this age when the Gospel is preached among men it will have a mixed reception. There will be varied types of reaction, from no impression at all to full and faithful response. Every preacher's experience has verified this prophecy.

The parable of the tares foresees the mixed condition of the kingdom throughout this age. Along with the good there will be mingled the bad, the false, the imitation, the "cheat," and they cannot be separated until the end of the age. Again, experience has verified the prophecy.

The parable of the mustard seed has its significance in the unnatural, abnormal growth of this plant. It teaches that there will be an unnatural, abnormal growth in the outward church, in "Christendom," until it becomes a colossal, worldwide monstrosity more interested in politics than in spiritual salvation, a resting place for all sorts of the devil's "birds" (cf. v. 19). The modern "ecumenical movement" shouldn't surprise a Bible-believing Christian.

The parable of the leaven speaks of the insidious, pervading progress of evil in the "Christendom" of this interim age. The idea that this is the gradual growth of good throughout the world is unscriptural and un-natural: unscriptural because in the Bible leaven is always a symbol of evil, and unnatural because in nature evil is contagious, but good is not (compare measles, or a bad apple). The worldliness, hypocrisy, professionalism, ostentation, and indifference of the modern church are a part of Christ's prophetic preview of the church in our age.

The two parables of the hid treasure and the pearl of great price are frequently interpreted backward. Christ is the one who found and pur-chased these two treasures with everything He had. Probably the treasure hid in the field is Israel, and the pearl is the church. Christ gave His very life to redeem them. These parables point to the basic fact that underlies this whole age of grace, the cross of Christ.

The last of the mystery parables deals with the end of the age, when there will be an ultimate time of separation, when the mixed-up condition of this age will be brought to an end, the good will be gathered in, the bad will be destroyed. It assures us that there will be an end to this present mystery form of the kingdom.

II. The Purpose and Program of the Church Age

Many criticisms of the church are based on unscriptural notions of its purpose, and many failures in church work are due to a misunderstanding of its program. Two passages of Scripture need to be reviewed.

1. **Matthew 16:18.** Jesus said, "I will build my church." The context before and after relates this statement to the change in Jesus' ministry and message which resulted from His rejection by the Jews. It follows soon after the parables of the mystery of the kingdom, and it is immediately followed by a plain announcement of a change in Jesus' message. "From that time forth began Jesus to shew unto his disciples, how that he must go unto Jerusalem, and suffer . . . and be killed, and be raised again" (16:21). This is the new program and message, now that rejection was certain and the postponement of the kingdom was in view. Jesus' message is, "I will build my church" (v. 18). "I will come again in my kingdom" (vv. 27-28).

Of the many truths in this passage, perhaps the most significant for our present purpose is the assurance of success it expresses. Christ, the Son of God, said it: "*I* will build *my* church." In spite of all the talk about the failures of the church, the church actually is not failing. Christ is building His church, and He is succeeding in this task. Only when we mistakenly assign to the church a purpose which it is not intended to perform can we say that it is failing. For example, some think that the purpose of the church is to build the kingdom of God. When judged on the basis of this false purpose, it seems to fail. Certainly it is not succeeding in building a kingdom of God on earth. Or, some think the purpose of the church is to win the world to Christ. According to this standard, too, the church is failing, for actual statistics show that unbelievers are increasing faster than believers, and we are losing the race. There are more unsaved people in the world today than there were last year, more than there were when Jesus spoke these words. But the church is not failing. It was never intended to win the world to Christ, but to call out *some* of the world to Christ. It is succeeding in that. Some say the purpose of the church is to evangelize the world, to *offer* salvation to all. Let us be very careful here, lest we misunderstand. If that is the purpose of the church, then it is failing; and it cannot fail, for Jesus said, "I will build my church." Evangelizing the world is the *program* of the church, it is the method we use to accomplish our purpose, but our *purpose* is to call out some, and that is being done. Christ is assaulting the strongholds of Satan and snatching as brands from the burning the material out of which He is building His church. And the gates of hell shall not prevail against it. It will succeed. It is succeeding, because He is doing it.

2. **Acts 15:14-17.** In this important passage the presiding pastor of the Jerusalem church council closes their discussion of the problem of how to admit Gentile believers into the church by setting forth God's purpose for this age. He relates how God "at the first did visit the Gentiles, to take out of them a people for his name," as witnessed by Peter's experience at Caesarea and Paul's successful missionary journeys. Then he quotes an Old Testament prophecy, saying, "After this I will return, and will build again the tabernacle of David, which is fallen down." The words "after this" seem to refer to the successful ministry of the Gospel to the Gentiles; after this age of grace, in which God is calling out a people for His name, then Christ will return to reestablish and restore Israel and David's prophesied kingdom. Thus we have an outline of God's purposes: (1) the present age, in which God is building His church of called-out ones, (2) the return of Christ, and (3) the resumption of His dealings with Israel.

III. The Course of This Age

Frequently the New Testament describes for us the moral and spiritual trends of the present age, showing us what conditions will be like in "the last days."

1. **The meaning of the term "the last days."** In the Old Testament this expression and a similar one, "the latter days," were used to refer to the prophesied future, the end time, the day of the Lord, the times of the Messiah. This usage certainly carries over into the New Testament, referring now, of course, to the second coming of Christ and its related events (John 6:39; 11:24; 12:48). Sometimes, however, it seems to refer to the entire period of the church age (for example, Acts 2:17; Heb. 1:2; I John 2:18). This is not strange when we realize that the Old Testament made no distinction between the first and second coming of Christ, and even in the New Testament it was never dreamed that the interval between would stretch out to nineteen centuries. The early Christians rightly thought of Christ's return as being soon. They were in "the last days." The last days thus began with Christ's first coming, and continue until He comes again. However, since this period has stretched out so greatly, as we come closer to its end, we may expect that the "last day" conditions which are true of the whole age will become increasingly pertinent to the last of these last

days.

2. **II Timothy 3:1-9.** This is not the only significant passage dealing with these last days (cf. I Tim. 4:1; II Peter 3:3; Jude 18) but it is one of the fullest. In accord with what we have just said, it describes conditions during this whole church age. They were true in Paul's day; he uses the present tense concerning them (v. 8). But he also uses the future tense (v. 1, "shall come"), and he expects them to become more and more evil as the age continues (v. 13). So it seems proper to consider this passage as a prophecy of conditions as they will exist at the end of the present church age.

Two conditions stand out in this passage which will mark the course of our age and particularly its end. First, we can expect that evil will increase and abound, that the end of the age will see a breakdown of moral and spiritual standards. The best commentary on these verses is your daily newspaper. Lovers of self . . . covetous . . . disobedient to parents . . . unthankful . . . without natural affection . . . despisers of the good . . . lovers of pleasure . . . having a form of godliness, but without power or reality . . . ever learning, never coming to truth . . . corrupt minds. Compare this list to the moral conditions as you know them in your town. Surely here is an example of prophecy being fulfilled.

The second condition reflected here is the prevalence of false teachers, and an apostate religious system. They have the outward form or appearance of godliness, but they deny its power. They lead captive, they withstand the truth, they are seducers, they deceive others and they are deceived themselves. Peter speaks of these: "There shall come in the last days scoffers, walking after their own lusts, and saying, Where is the promise of his coming?" (II Peter 3:3-4). Jude reminds us of Peter's prophecy and adds his own powerful denunciations of these apostate, false teachers. So this is what prophecy leads us to expect will become increasingly true as this age draws to a close. Already it seems so bad that it cannot get worse, but it will.

IV. A Prophetic Outline of Church History.

Here we turn to Revelation, chapters 2 and 3, a most remarkable portion of God's prophetic Word. It consists of seven short letters addressed to seven churches in Asia Minor. They are dictated by Christ himself from heaven to the apostle John on the isle of Patmos, and make the beginning of his great prophetic Book of the Revelation. We believe they are the clearest and fullest of all prophecies regarding the church and the progress of the church age.

1. **The interpretation of these seven letters.** First, these are seven letters to seven actual, historical churches of that time. Some of them are mentioned elsewhere in the New Testament; some are not. All these seven cities were prominent places in that time, and there is no reason to doubt that these were real letters to real churches.

Second, these were seven churches chosen because they represented seven different types or conditions of churches in that time and in every time. The number seven is significant, particularly in the Book of Revelation, indicating the full or complete number, and therefore these seven are typical of all churches. There were then, and still are, churches like the Ephesian church, like the Smyrna church, and so forth. The characteristics marked in these seven are typical of seven types of churches found in all ages, including our own.

Third, these are prophetic of seven periods of the history of the church through this church age. Not all Bible students agree on this last point, but I believe it is a true one. The place of these letters in this prophetic book suggests a prophetic significance, and the remarkable manner in which they really do fit the pattern of actual history seems too close to be coincidental. So, along with most other premillennialists, I see in these seven churches an outline of seven periods in the history of this age, the first of which was characterized by the church at Ephesus, the second period by the church at Smyrna, and so on. Thus the last period of this church age, just before the second coming of Christ, will be characterized by the church at Laodicea, the church to whom the seventh and last letter was written.

2. **The Laodicean period of the church.** When we compare this prophetic outline with actual developments in the history of the church age, it seems clear that we are now in the Laodicean period. And this conviction is deepened when we notice its characteristics.

First, it is neither cold nor hot, but lukewarm. To be cold in religious things is to be unresponsive, perhaps even hostile. To be hot in religious things is to be enthusiastic, on fire, all-out, putting God first without hesitation or reserve. To be lukewarm is to be in between. The lukewarm Christian goes to church; he enjoys the services; he is not unresponsive. But he doesn't get *too* interested, he wouldn't let his religion interfere with his other activities.

Second, the Laodiceans consider themselves rich and needing nothing. They have just completed an elaborate new sanctuary with stained glass windows and plush carpets, an architectural design that has won the acclaim of national trade magazines. Their pastor is prominent in all civic activities and much in demand as a dynamic after-dinner speaker. They have a minister of music, a minister of education, a paid choir, paid soloists, paid ushers. Of course, they don't have any prayer meeting, what is there to pray for? You can fill in the rest of the picture.

Third, the Laodiceans are actually most miserable and poor and needy, but so spiritually blind that they do not realize their need. They are spiritual paupers, with all their treasures in the "bank" down here. They are blind to spiritual values, unable to appreciate the riches in Christ which they are missing. They are naked, dressed as they are in their own opinions of themselves, not knowing that their sins are naked and open before the eyes of Him with whom they have to do.

Fourth, they are shutting Christ outside their church and their lives. It is a tragic picture: Christ's name on the bulletin board, Christ's cross on the steeple, but no Christ within! He is standing at the door, knocking, promising to enter if anyone will open to Him. The situation of the church seems to be past remedy; there is no hope for it. But still the offer goes out to individuals in these lukewarm, materially prosperous, spiritually destitute churches, to open the door of their hearts and let Him come in.

Such is the picture prophecy paints of the church in the end time.

SUMMARY

The Bible gives us a prophetic description of conditions in the church and in the world during this church age.

It is a picture of progressive deterioration in moral and spiritual standards. Even the outward church is to become indifferent and apostate.

In the midst of this the true church is succeeding in its God-given purpose, calling out a people for His name.

9

The Resurrection in Prophecy

INTRODUCTION

Resurrection is one of the great facts of the future and a part of Bible prophecy. Already we have dealt in part with one aspect of the subject, in our study of the Rapture of the church. But we need to see it as it relates to other groups, and how it fits into the prophetic program of the future.

THE AIM

A study on the resurrection ought to impress us anew with the importance and significance of the human body as a permanent part of our human personality, and the need to keep it pure. While we will be dealing with many details about the time and the order and the extent of the resurrection as they fit into the future, one should always keep in mind the sobering fact: I am going to live in this body for eternity.

THE DEVELOPMENT

First, we need to make clear in our thinking what we mean by resurrection, particularly since many unscriptural notions about it are prevalent.

Second, we shall look at John 5:28-29, a passage which deals with the fact and extent of resurrection.

Third, we shall study I Corinthians 15:22-24, a passage which deals with the order and time of the resurrections.

Fourth, we shall deal with several passages which describe "the first resurrection."

Fifth, we shall study the chief passage referring to the final resurrection.

THE EXPOSITION

I. The Meaning of Resurrection

This is among those words which are so familiar and common that we often assume folks know what they mean when in reality they may know very little, or even have completely wrong notions, about them. Actually, its meaning in the Scriptures is very simple. It means coming back to life. The original from which it is translated is a word meaning literally "to stand up," or "to cause to stand up, to raise up." For a dead person to stand up is to come back to life.

This idea must be carefully distinguished from the idea of the continuation of life or existence beyond death, or the so-called "immortality of the soul." When the Bible speaks of resurrection, it does not mean that the person "lives on" in another world; it means he comes back to life in this world. Resurrection is the reversal of death. When a person dies, his body and spirit are separated. In the resurrection his body and spirit are reunited. This involves the raising up out of the grave and bringing back to life of that dead body. So resurrection in the Bible is "bodily resurrection." There is no such thing as a "spiritual resurrection"; such an expression is a contradiction in terms.

Sometimes the term "spiritual resurrection" is used when the term should more properly be metaphorical or figurative resurrection. The Bible does use the word in connection with two ideas where the word obviously has this metaphorical or figurative sense. One of these is the "resurrection" of national Israel, or the restoration of Israel to their national identity after their seeming deadness for so many centuries (Ezek. 37). The other is the newness of life in Christ which belongs to the Christian (Rom. 6:3-11; Eph. 2:1, 5). But this figurative use of the term does not take the place of the natural and physical sense, for Romans 8:11 shows that our mortal bodies will yet be made alive, even though we already have newness of life in Christ.

II. The Extent of the Resurrection (John 5:28-29)

These words of Jesus obviously assert the *fact* of a resurrection. "All that are in the graves shall hear . . . and shall come forth." Jesus elsewhere repeatedly states this as a plain fact (see John 6:39, 40, 44; 11:23-26), even refuting the Sadducees, who did not believe in a resurrection (Matt. 22:23-33). Also these words support what we have said before regarding the *nature* of the resurrection, that it has to do with the *bodies,* for those that are "in the graves" will come forth. But our purpose in looking at these verses here is to see what Jesus taught as to the *extent* of the resurrection. Whom all will it include?

1. **The resurrection will include all the dead.** Verse 28 says "all that are in the graves." Verse 25 says "the dead." In some of the passages used above, the reference is to the saved only (John 6:40, and others). But this is not the case here, for Jesus specifically includes those who have done good and those who have done evil (5:29). So the resurrection will be general, in the sense that it will include *all*.

2. **The resurrection will be in two parts.** Verse 29 clearly distinguishes two groups of people and two resurrections. The one group, composed of those who have done good, will come forth unto the resurrection of life; the other group, composed of those who have done evil, unto the resurrection of damnation. So the resurrection will *not* be general in the sense that all are raised up alike at the same time. There will be *two* resurrections.

III. The Order of the Resurrection (I Cor. 15:22-24)

Again this passage insists that all will be raised (v. 22), but we want to look particularly at the teaching of this passage on the *order,* or successive stages, of the resurrection. "Every man in his own order" (v. 23). The word "order" means a rank, and pictures the resurrection as taking place in stages, with each stage including those of a certain rank, or class. Paul mentioned three of these ranks.

1. **Christ, the firstfruits.** The resurrection of Christ was the first resurrection and was in a class of its own. Since His resurrection is past and has been studied many times in other connections, we shall not include this in our present study, except to note that the term "firstfruits" implies that

His resurrection is the guarantee and sample of those following.

2. **Those that are Christ's at His coming**. Comparing this passage with John 5, we see that this second rank is "the resurrection of life." Later we shall see that it is called "the first resurrection." It includes "those that are Christ's," an expression which we believe includes all the saved of all ages. The time of this resurrection is fixed "at his coming," that is, at His second coming.

3. **The end resurrection**. The third rank is stated in the words, "Then cometh the end." The original makes it clear that this is another rank in the list; "then" might better be translated "next." The time for this rank of the resurrection is fixed as after the kingdom, "when he shall have delivered up the kingdom to God." Christ will rule in His earthly messianic kingdom for a specific period of time (elsewhere we are told it is one thousand years), until all enemies are subdued. The last enemy to be subdued will be death itself. But since the saved dead have already been raised in the second rank, "the dead" now includes only the rest, the unsaved dead. This, then, is the "resurrection of damnation" mentioned by Jesus.

IV. The First Resurrection

We look now more particularly at one of these stages of the resurrection, the resurrection of life, as Jesus called it, and see its relation to prophetic events.

1. **The Rapture resurrection** (I Thess. 4:13-17; I Cor. 15:50-54). In our study of the Rapture we learned that one of the major events to take place then will be the resurrection of all those who "sleep in Jesus," the "dead in Christ." At the end of this church age, when the trumpet sounds and the Lord Jesus Christ descends from heaven to catch up to himself His own saints, "the dead in Christ shall rise first." Note that Paul is talking about the physical resurrection of their bodies, for he speaks of them as "asleep" and "dead"; yet they come with Him from heaven. When a Christian dies, his body is laid in the grave, where it sleeps; it is dead. But the spirit goes immediately to be with Christ in heaven (II Cor. 5:6-8; Phil. 1:23). When Christ returns, these spirits of the saved ones who have died will be brought back from heaven with Him (I Thess. 4:14). Then will take

place the resurrection; the dead in Christ will rise. Their bodies will come out of the graves, will be rejoined with their spirits, and alive again they will share the rest of the events of the Rapture along with those who have not died.

The I Corinthians 15 passage explains that this resurrection is more than a mere bringing back to physical life. It is that, but it is more. The resurrected body is the same body as the one buried, but it is changed, so that now it is immortal (it will never die again) and it is incorruptible (no more polluted by the presence of sin). This is necessary before we can inherit the kingdom of God (v. 50). So Paul goes on to explain that even the saints who are still alive when Christ comes, although they will never die and therefore will never be resurrected (only a dead person can be brought back to life), yet they must experience this same transformation from corruption to incorruption. So he says, "Behold, I shew you a mystery [something never before told]; we shall not all sleep [some will not die, those who are alive when Jesus comes], but we shall all be changed [transformed so that we, too, have the same incorruptible, immortal body as the resurrected saints have received]" (v. 51).

2. **The tribulation saints** (Rev. 20:4-6). Here we have another reference to resurrection in connection with the coming of Christ. Chapter 19 of Revelation has just described the great second advent of Christ in power and glory, His destruction of His enemies, the taking of the Antichrist and the False Prophet, the binding of Satan. Then John goes on (v. 4) to speak of thrones and those who sat on them. In this connection he makes special mention of one group, the martyrs who died at the hands of Antichrist during the tribulation period. Of them he says, "And they lived [in the original Greek: they came to life] and reigned with Christ a thousand years." Here is the resurrection of the saints of the tribulation period, which takes place at Christ's coming.

Verse 5 goes on, "The rest of the dead lived not again until the thousand years were finished. This is the first resurrection." So the Book of Revelation divides the resurrection into two parts: (1) the first resurrection, which takes place at the coming of Christ and before the one thousand years, and (2) the rest of the dead, after the one thousand years. This is the same division Paul made when he listed "those that are Christ's at his coming, *then* cometh the end," and the same that Jesus referred to when

He mentioned the resurrection of life and the resurrection of damnation.

It seems obvious that this first resurrection includes two groups of saved people: (1) those saints of the church age who are His at His coming for the Rapture, and (2) the saints of the tribulation period who are His at His coming at the Revelation. Revelation 20:6 shows that these of the first resurrection "shall be priests of God and of Christ, and shall reign with him a thousand years," facts which are true also of the church of this age.

3. **The Old Testament saints** (Dan. 12:1-2). Here is described a resurrection of yet another group of saved folks, the godly Jews of the Old Testament dispensation. "Many of them that sleep in the dust of the earth shall awake, some to everlasting life, and some to shame and everlasting contempt" (v. 2). A better translation would be, "And many from among the sleepers of the dust of the earth shall awake: these [who awake] shall be unto everlasting life, but those [the rest of the sleepers, who do not awake then] shall be unto shame and everlasting contempt."

Verse 1 makes it clear that this resurrection of the godly Jews will follow the time of trouble and the deliverance of the living Jews. In other words, this resurrection of the Old Testament saints coincides in time with the first resurrection of Revelation 20.

It seems then, that the first resurrection includes *all* the saved: (1) the saints of the church age, at the Rapture, (2) the saints of the tribulation period, and (3) the saints of the Old Testament, at the Revelation.

V. The End Resurrection (Rev. 20:11-15)

Jesus, it will be remembered, spoke of a resurrection of damnation for those who have done evil. Paul spoke of an "end" resurrection, after the kingdom, which would complete the resurrection of all ranks. John said, "The rest of the dead [that is, the unsaved] lived not again until the thousand years were finished" (Rev. 20:5). We look now to this final resurrection.

This is the account of the Great White Throne judgment. It is located in time at the end of the thousand years of the millennial reign of Christ on the earth. Immediately following it John introduces a new heaven and a new earth (Rev. 21:1), the eternal estate. Our present interest in this judgment is to note *who* will appear there.

Verse 12 of chapter 20 says: "I saw the dead, small and great, stand before God . . . and the dead were judged. . . ." When we seek to identify these dead, we are left in no doubt, for verse 5 said: "The rest of the dead lived not again until the thousand years were finished"; that is, until this Great White Throne Judgment, which comes when the thousand years are finished. So "the dead" of verse 12 are "the rest of the dead" of verse 5, those who did not participate in the first resurrection. In our study of this first resurrection we learned that it included *all* the *saved* who have died. The rest of the dead, then, includes only the wicked, the unsaved. They are the only ones not previously resurrected.

Verse 13 further identifies them by telling from whence they come. "The sea" and "death" and "hell" (Hades) gave up the dead which were in them. "Hades" is the place where the *spirits* of unsaved men go when they die (Luke 16:22-23). "The sea" could only be the depository of the bodies of those who died there and thus were not placed in the grave. It would appear, then, that the third term, "death," is used here to mean the grave. So this resurrection gathers the bodies of the unsaved dead from the sea (those not buried) and from the grave (those buried), and gathers their souls from Hades. Then, as resurrection always means, their souls or spirits reunite with their bodies and they come to life again, in the flesh, to stand before God in judgment.

It should be clear that these resurrection bodies are not like the resurrection bodies which resulted from the first resurrection. They are not immortal. Verse 14 goes on to describe the outcome of this judgment. "Death and hell [that is, the bodies and spirits of the dead; or all that come forth out of these two realms] were cast into the lake of fire. This is the *second death*." Since they die again they are not immortal. Neither are they incorruptible, for they stand before God in all the sins found written in the books. There is only one source from which a soul may find relief from its sin and corruption; that is the blood of the Lamb. But these are not found written in the Lamb's book of life. Their lot instead is corruption itself, "where their worm dieth not, and the fire is not quenched."

Dear reader, where do you stand? Is Jesus Christ your Saviour? Just think "God so loved the world, that he gave his only begotten Son, that whosoever believeth in him *should not* perish, but have everlasting life." We have presented here what it will mean to perish, and in contrast what it will mean to have everlasting life. "Blessed and holy is he that hath part in the first resurrection: on such the second death hath no power, but they shall be priests of God and of Christ, and shall reign with him a thousand years" (Rev. 20:6).

SUMMARY

Every man, woman, and child who has ever lived and died on this earth, from Adam to the end of human history, is going to come to life again in the body.

Those who are saved, from all ages, will be raised at the second coming of Christ. They will constitute three groups: (1) The Christians of this present age, the church, will be raised at the time of the Rapture, when Christ comes to catch away His people before the tribulation. (2) Those who are saved during the seven-year tribulation period and martyred by Antichrist will be resurrected at Christ's second coming in glory to establish His kingdom. (3) The saints of the Old Testament dispensation will be raised also at the coming of Christ to set up His kingdom.

The rest of the dead, or all the unsaved who have ever died, will remain in their graves and in Hades until the end of the thousand-year reign of Christ. Then they will all be brought back to life so that they may stand before God in their bodies to be judged. They all will be cast into the lake of fire, which is called the second death, and will remain there forever.

10

The Judgments in Prophecy

SUGGESTED BACKGROUND DEVOTIONAL READING

Monday—Christ Bore Our Judgment (II Cor. 5:14-21)
Tuesday—Believer Judging Himself (I Cor. 11:27-32)
Wednesday—Believer's Works Judged (I Cor. 3:10-15)
Thursday—Nations To Be Judged (Matt. 25:31-46)
Friday—Israel To Be Judged (Ezek. 20:33-44)
Saturday—Great White Throne Judgment (Rev. 20:11-15)
Sunday—Angels That Sinned (II Peter 2:4-9; Jude 6)

INTRODUCTION

Most people who are at all familiar with religious subjects have a general notion that the Bible teaches a judgment day is coming. But their ideas about the nature of that judgment are very vague and usually quite wrong. What *does* the Bible teach about judgment? Actually there are many judgments spoken of in the Scriptures. Not all of these are related to the subject of prophecy, for some of them are past and some are present. There are some which are future, and in this chapter we will seek to relate these to the framework of prophetic truth. Since, however, the whole subject is so widely misunderstood, we shall include a brief statement of those which are not prophetic in nature.

THE AIM

Our first aim will be to learn what the Bible says about these judgments. But, even more important, our aim will be to bring the lesson of these judgments to bear on each of our lives. These future events are not merely facts about which we are curious. They are realities we face, which should influence our decisions and actions.

THE DEVELOPMENT

First, we shall briefly review the past and present judgments which are not strictly related to our prophetic study. We shall discover that they are probably the most important judgments of all!

Turning to the judgments of the future, we shall, second, study those judgments which determine entrance into the messianic kingdom: the judgment of Israel and the judgment of the nations.

Third, we shall consider those judgments which determine eternal rewards and punishments: the Judgment Seat of Christ and the Great White Throne Judgment.

THE EXPOSITION

I. The Judgments of the Past and of the Present

1. **The judgment that determines a person's eternal destiny.** It may be a surprise that the judgment which determines the soul's eternal destiny is not future at all; it has already taken place. The popular notion is that sometime in the dim future Gabriel will blow his horn, all men will stand before a huge throne, and God will judge each one according to the life he has lived. He will put all the good things we have done on one side of the scales and all the bad things on the other side, while we hold our breath watching the balances teeter this way and that until they stop. If the good outweighs the bad, the Lord will say, "Congratulations! You made it. Come on in." If the bad outweighs the good, then the word will be, "Sorry, you'll have to take your place below." This idea is completely wrong. There isn't anything in all the Bible which teaches such a concept of judgment.

In John 12:31 Jesus said, "Now is the judgment of this world." He went on to speak of being lifted up from the earth, and John explains, "This he said, signifying what death he should die" (v. 33). So the judgment of the world took place on the cross of Calvary. There sin was judged; there a plan of salvation was wrought. There the destinies of all men were settled. From that cross there is a crossroad, one road leading to heaven and one to hell. We face this judgment when we are presented with the gospel message of the cross. Our destiny is fixed on the basis of what we do with the Christ of the cross. If we believe and receive Him, we are saved, our judgment is past, our destiny is fixed, we have everlasting life, we are on the road that leads to heaven. If we refuse to believe and reject Him, we are lost, our judgment is past, our destiny is sure, we are on the road that ends in hell. *We* decide where we are going to spend eternity, by our response to this judgment of the cross (read John 3:16-18, 36; 5:24).

2. **The judgment that determines a believer's chastening or blessing**. In I Corinthians 11:30-32 Paul speaks of a present judgment of the believer. In a context which speaks of responsibility to participate in the communion service in a worthy manner, Paul makes the startling statement that because of sin in this matter many of the Corinthian Christians were being afflicted with physical sickness by the Lord, and some even had fallen into the sleep of physical death. Then he says, "If we would judge ourselves, we should not be judged [of the Lord]." This judgment which we might avoid by self-judgment is the chastening of the Lord. Here, then, is a present judgment of the believer's sins. Its purpose is to get rid of our sins. If we judge ourselves, and deal with our sins in the appointed manner, God's purpose for our lives will be realized. If we do not judge ourselves, God will have to judge our sins by bringing His chastening upon us.

How much of the trouble and unhappiness of the Christian could be avoided if we learned the lesson of this judgment!

II. The Judgments Which Determine Entrance into the Kingdom

There is much in prophecy to connect judgment with the messianic kingdom of the future. That great golden age to come is to be introduced by "the day of the Lord." This day of the Lord is a major topic in most of the prophets' messages, and always it is pictured as a day of judgment from God upon the sinful world, preceding the setting up of His glorious kingdom. These judgments fall on both the people of Israel and the rest of the world. God's people, before they can be blessed with the establishment of the promised kingdom, must be purged from the sins which have separated them from God and have driven them out of their land into worldwide exile. The Gentile world, too, must be punished for their mistreatment of Israel, their rejection of the true God, and their idolatry. This judgment of Israel is called "the time of Jacob's trouble," "the great tribulation," and we have spoken of it at some length in previous lessons. The judgment of the Gentile nations, too, has been dealt with.

But aside from this period of judgment, chastening, and punishment which belongs to the day of the Lord, the Bible speaks of two specific events which may be called judgments, by which it is determined who will enter into the messianic kingdom.

1. **The judgment of Israel**. In the midst of this terrible time of judgment

when Israel is being punished and purged through her cruel experiences under the Antichrist, God himself plans and brings to pass a day of judgment for Israel. It is referred to in many of the passages describing the return of the Jews to Palestine and the coming of the Messiah. We have selected one of these, Ezekiel 20:33-38, for our present study.

Several steps are outlined here of God's dealings with His people.

a. God will bring them out of the nations where they have been scattered (vv. 33-34).

b. He will bring them into "the wilderness of the people" (v. 35). The location of this wilderness is not identified. In verse 36 He compares this experience with the wilderness wanderings of Israel after the exodus from Egypt. Revelation 12 also speaks of Israel (the "woman" of the allegory) as fleeing into the wilderness, where she is preserved from Satan's wrath for the last half of this tribulation week. Perhaps the wilderness of Edom, Ammon, and Moab are the places referred to (cf. Dan. 11:41).

c. God will plead with them there "face to face," as He pleaded with their fathers in the wilderness, or at Sinai. This suggests a direct, personal encounter, probably by the personal presence of the Messiah himself, offering them the opportunity to look on Him and be saved.

d. God will cause them to "pass under the rod" (v. 37). A similar expression in Jeremiah 33:13 would indicate that this term means to count them, as a shepherd counts his own sheep, and to include them in His own flock. The last part of verse 37 would agree with this: "I will bring you into the bond of the covenant."

e. God will "purge out from among you the rebels, and them that transgress against me" (v. 38). It would seem that this does not refer to those who have rebelled and transgressed in the past, for *all* Israel has been doing that, but those who at this occasion refuse to be brought under the bond of the covenant, or refuse to acknowledge and receive the Messiah. These He "will purge out." All will be brought out of the countries where they were scattered, but those who rebel "shall not enter into the land of Israel." Evidently this purging of the rebellious will mean that they die there in the wilderness, as their fathers who rebelled under Moses died in the wilderness.

Verses 40-44 make it clear that this is a judgment which determines who shall enter the messianic kingdom. Just as those who failed to pass this judgment were not permitted to enter the land, so those who pass it are now described as being in the land, accepted of the Lord, and worshiping Him (v. 40). And again it speaks of these who are permitted to enter the land as the ones who have repented of their former sins and recognized God's gracious dealings in their salvation.

Where does this judgment of Israel fit in chronologically? This is a question which I believe cannot be answered dogmatically. It certainly belongs very close to the actual setting up of Messiah's kingdom. It seems to the present writer that the reference to the bringing back of *all* of the scattered nation of Israel, and the personal encounter with God described in verse 35, would place it *after* the second advent of Christ and during those few days mentioned in Daniel 12:12, probably speaking of the organizational period necessary at the start of the Millennium.

2. **The judgment of the nations (Gentiles).** Not only is the nation of Israel judged to see who shall enter the Messiah's kingdom, but such a judgment is necessary also for the Gentile world. Messiah's kingdom will include all nations; therefore there must be some Gentiles who will enter it. This judgment is described in Matthew 25:31-46. Note several details.

a. The time of this judgment is made very clear: "When the Son of man shall come in his glory, and all the holy angels with him, *then* shall he sit upon the throne of his glory" (v. 31). Thus, this judgment follows immediately, or very quickly, after Christ's second coming to establish His kingdom.

b. The persons involved in this judgment are "all nations" (v. 32). The word is used in contrast to Jews and usually is translated "Gentiles." So this judgment involves "all Gentiles." When we read it this way it avoids a misconception often created that these "nations" are national units, such as Egypt, Germany, the United States. (That this is not the case is seen also by comparing it with Matthew 28:19, where we are to make disciples of, and baptize, "all nations.") If we read this passage apart from any preconceived, unscriptural notions of a "future general judgment," I believe it will be clear that this judgment deals only with the "living" Gentiles. There is not a hint in the entire passage which would suggest the dead. In other words, when Messiah comes and sets up His kingdom, He will judge all the Gentiles *of that time,* the ones who must be dealt with in the task of setting up His worldwide government.

c. He divides them into two groups *on the basis of their own identity* (v. 33). The imagery used is that of a shepherd, so one group is termed sheep, the other goats. But this judgment doesn't make one a sheep and another a goat. They *are* that before they come. This judgment merely separates them and assigns them to their respective fates. This is not a judgment which makes salvation or destiny depend on works. What they have done, either good or bad, is used as an explanation of how one can tell their real nature, but it does not make them either sheep or goats.

d. The reward for the "sheep" Gentiles is entrance into the messianic kingdom (v. 34). This is not "heaven," but the earthly, real kingdom foretold by the prophets, to be set up when the Messiah comes. In that kingdom the whole world will be included. This judgment is separating out which Gentiles will be permitted to enter it.

e. The judgment for the "goat" Gentiles will be everlasting destruction in an eternal hell of fire (v. 41). In other words, those Gentiles who do not stand this test will be shut out of the kingdom. They will die and as wicked dead will ultimately end up at the Great White Throne Judgment and the lake of fire. While it is not specifically stated *how* they will die, it might be assumed that the very pronouncement of their doom by the King would bring about their execution, just as the multitudes of their contemporaries at the battle of Armageddon will die from the "sword that proceedeth out of the mouth" of that same King.

f. The basis of distinction between these two groups at this judgment is their treatment of the King and His "brethren" (vv. 35-40; 42-45). Here the King identifies himself so completely with certain ones whom He calls His "brethren" that their treatment of these constitutes also their treatment of Him. Unknown even to themselves, these Gentiles have been demonstrating their true nature and character by the way they have reacted to the needs of Christ's brethren. Again, let it be clear that this is not salvation by works. Their treatment of these brethren has simply revealed their true natures. If their nature was right with God, if they were saved, they acted like such by showing kindness to God's people. If they were rebellious toward God, if they were unsaved, they acted like such by failing to show kindness.

Who are these "brethren"? From the context in Matthew 24 and 25, and from its setting at the end of the time of Jacob's trouble, it has been insisted by some that the brethren are the Jewish people. Thus, the Gentiles of the tribulation period will be judged on the basis of their attitude toward the Jews; the unpardonable sin of that time will be anti-Semitism. Personally I am convinced that this is too narrow an interpretation. Certainly not *all* Jews, nor Israel as a *nation,* are the "brethren" referred to here, for unbelieving Jews are at this very moment undergoing the judgment of God himself, and even God is not showing kindness to them. Also it must be remembered that Jesus had said, "Whosoever shall do the will of my Father which is in heaven, the same is my brother, and sister, and mother" (Matt. 12:50). There are others in this tribulation period who have been doing the will of the Father, as well as the Jews. So I would hold that the "brethren" referred to here are *all* of God's believers in that end time, believing Jews and believing Gentiles. Gentiles who have shown kindness to the 144,000 Jews and to the innumerable multitude of Gentile believers in their persecutions, will by those acts of kindness have demonstrated that they do not belong to Antichrist's crowd, that they rather are God's people. As such they will enter the kingdom. Those who refuse such kindness demonstrate their support of Antichrist's program and their rebellion against God. As such they cannot enter the kingdom.

At this point, please look at John 3:3 and 5. Very definitely Jesus says that no one can enter the kingdom except he be born again. The Old Testament also insisted that only those right with God would enter that kingdom. Therefore, it must be understood that the "sheep" of Matthew 25 are born-again individual Gentiles living when Christ comes, who will be permitted to enter the kingdom age.

III. The Judgments that Determine Eternal Rewards and Punishments

Two more future judgments are described in the Bible. Neither of these is for the purpose of determining destiny. That judgment is past. These are for the purpose of determining what each individual's condition will be in his self-determined destiny.

1. **The Bema Seat Judgment of Christ**. There are many references to this "judgment seat of Christ" (Rom. 14:10; II Cor. 5:10). Its clearest and fullest presentation is in I Corinthians 3:13-15, and it is frequently the subject of sermon or Bible study. Here we shall merely review its main features and relate it to its proper place in the prophetic program.

a. This is a judgment of works (v. 13). Second Corinthians 5:10 says, "That every one may receive the things done in his body, according to that he hath done, whether it be good or bad." Its purpose is to determine rewards and punishments. The believer will be rewarded for his good deeds and will suffer loss for his evil deeds. Of course, there is no penal infliction here, for the Bible teaches clearly that the believer is justified and will never come into condemnation. Note I Corinthians 3:15: "He himself shall be saved; yet so as by fire"—saved like a man snatched out of a burning house, with all his goods lost.

b. This judgment will determine the saved man's condition, or status, or degree of blessedness in heaven. The Bible speaks of many rewards, sometimes referring to them as crowns. This judgment of works will determine just how many or how much of these each individual Christian will enjoy in heaven. We are going to reign with Christ in the millennial kingdom. Perhaps one will be told, "Rule thou over ten cities," another five, and so forth.

c. This judgment will take place when the Lord comes (I Cor. 4:5). Frequently the Bible speaks of the coming of Christ as the time of rewards (Rev. 22:12; James 5:7-8; II Tim. 4:8). For the believer of this church age the coming of the Lord means the Rapture. So the judgment of the believer's works at the Judgment Seat of Christ must take place just after the Rapture of the church. Since the church is in heaven during that time, the scene of this judgment must be in heaven.

2. **The Great White Throne Judgment** (Rev. 20:11-15). Already in a previous chapter we have studied this subject, and here it needs only to be placed in its proper prophetic framework.

a. This also is a judgment of works (v. 13). Its purpose is to determine the degree of punishment to be meted out to those who appear there. There is no reward, for those who stand there are the rest of the dead who did not take part in the first resurrection, which included all the saved. While the Lamb's book of life is there, it seems only to be for the purpose of showing who is *not* in it (v. 15).

b. This judgment will determine the degree of punishment a man will receive in hell. Perhaps this may be a surprise to some, but the Bible clearly teaches it. All sinners who are not saved by faith in Jesus Christ will be punished in hell. But some are worse sinners than others, and their suffering will therefore be greater than that of others (read Luke 12:46-48). Since hell is eternal, and those who go there will all stay there forever, the difference is not in the length of their punishment but in its degree. Just how this difference will be made is not told.

c. This judgment of the works of the lost will take place at the end of the millennial kingdom, when time will pass into eternity and the eternal estate will begin. Thus it waits until the last sinner on earth from all its ages has died, and the company of the lost is complete. Then they will all be raised and stand before their Judge.

SUMMARY

The Bible speaks of many judgments, only some of which are yet future and belong to the subject of prophecy.

The judgment which determines whether a person will go to heaven or to hell is already past, and each person decides his own destiny by what he does with Christ and His claims upon his life.

There will be judgments on the people who are living when Christ comes back to set up His kingdom, to determine who may enter that blessed era. Only born-again people, both Jew and Gentile, may enter.

There will be judgments on the works of both saved and lost to determine the degree of blessing or punishment each individual is to experience in his eternal estate.

In the light of these solemn judgments, let each individual examine his own relation to God.

11

You in Prophecy

INTRODUCTION

This chapter might be titled "Fortunes Told!" Of course, every form of fortune-telling is condemned by the Bible, except the study of this predictive book, the Bible. But the Bible does tell us much about the future, as it relates to individuals of various types, so it is proper to "tell fortunes" by applying scriptural teachings.

THE AIM

Our aim in this chapter is twofold. First, we desire to review the major prophetic themes we have been studying, as we trace various individuals through the future events. Second, we hope to capture the personal interest of each reader, to see how these prophetic themes will involve him personally.

THE DEVELOPMENT

We shall simply try to trace in narrative form the *two* journeys through the future, one for the saved person and another for the unsaved. Each of you will determine which of the two courses you will follow.

From the nature of our subject, we shall not be studying specific Scripture passages. But at every step of the journey there are many passages which have formed the basis of this brief outline. Many of these have been included in the previous chapters.

THE EXPOSITION

I. The Rest of This Life

Starting right now, what does the future hold for *you*? You are now living your life in the flesh. You will go on living this physical life *for a while*.

How long will this period be? Bible prophecy doesn't fully answer that question, but your own common sense does. Prophecy says that the Lord may come at any moment to catch away His own, so the rest of this life as we now know it could be very short indeed. And beside this very real possibility there is the uncertainty of life itself. Who knows who will be the next to drop over with a heart attack? Certainly if we have any sense at all, one truth should *not* need emphasis today because it is so obvious. Life is very, very uncertain. What does the Bible say will happen to you during whatever time you may have left?

1. **For the saved person.** The course of your life during the rest of your time in the flesh, whether it be long or short, will be determined by your own choices and your own faithfulness to the Lord. You may make it a time of growth in grace and in the knowledge of the Lord. You may make it a blessed time of fellowship, walking close to the Lord and enjoying His presence. You may make it a profitable time, laying up for yourself treasures in heaven in the form of promised rewards for faithful service to the Lord. Or, you may neglect His grace, ignore His admonitions and pleadings, and live selfishly in your own way. If you do, as a child of God you will bring upon yourself the chastening of the Lord. He will have to rebuke your sin, purge your carnality, and prepare you for the place He has prepared for you. This is an unpleasant experience to go through, and it is unnecessary if you will let His indwelling Spirit work unhindered. But God must, and will, get us ready for our future as His own.

2. **For the unsaved person.** For you, too, the rest of this life is broadly described. In God's grace He may, for a while, continue to work in your heart by His Spirit, to bring conviction of sin and to lead you to Christ. But how long He will extend this opportunity we do not know. We know that each time you refuse the invitation of Christ it becomes harder to make that step. So for you the rest of this life will mean a dwindling opportunity to accept Christ. You may not suffer any terrible afflictions

from the Lord. Your life may be rather pleasant in a worldly sense. But remember, your increasing ease and contentment may be the gradual withdrawal of the Holy Spirit as He gives you up to your fate.

II. The End of This Life

How will this life as we now experience it come to an end?

1. **For the saved person.** There are two possibilities in the case of the child of God. a. Our blessed hope, the end of this life which we fervently expect and look forward to, is the coming of Christ to rapture us out of this life into His blessed presence. Just think of it! Right now as we sit reading, morning, afternoon, or night, or anytime before we die, we might feel within these mortal bodies a mysterious change taking place. Pain is gone. Weariness has disappeared. We hear the voice of our Lord calling, and up we go to meet Him in the air! This could happen at any moment.

b. Or if the Lord delays His coming, then we may be called upon to fall "asleep in Jesus." But for us the sting of death has been removed; the dread of it is gone. There will, of course, be the physical pain and suffering of the illness or accident which brings it about, but death itself cannot harm us one bit. For a while we will need to live apart from our bodies. They will be laid to rest in a grave. But we will be with our Lord! It will be just going to sleep and waking up in heaven, pain and sorrow and suffering behind, all glory ahead!

2. **For the unsaved person.** Again there are two possibilities. a. If the coming of the Lord and the Rapture take place while you are still living, it will mean that you are left behind to experience the events of the Great Tribulation period. But be sure of this: If you have been rejecting Christ now, you will continue to reject Him then. You will *not* be converted by that tremendous event, for it will simply serve to harden your unbelief. *Now* is the day of salvation.

b. If the Lord's coming is delayed, you will end this life by dying. Death, for you, will not be the sweet and quiet experience we have described for the Christian. You and he alike will undergo the physical suffering and pain involved in whatever manner of death may be your portion, but there the similarity ends. For you, death will mean the end of every good and pleasant experience. You have been enjoying life now, because of God's goodness to you. Think of all the things you count precious or worthwhile today. They will *all* be gone and done *forever*, the moment you die. You will never know another happy moment. Your body will be laid in the grave. Your spirit will go to the place God has prepared for the souls of the dead, called Hades or Sheol ("hell" in the King James Version). There you will be in torment, and you will remain there until the Great White Throne Judgment.

Once I saw on a church bulletin board: "If every living person knew what every dying man discovers five minutes after he dies, everyone would be saved today!"

III. During the Great Tribulation Period

What will be happening to individuals during this prophetic time-period?

1. **For the saved person.** The answer here is clear and simple. If you are a saved person, you will miss this terrible judgment time here on the earth. You will have been raptured out of this world before the judgment began. You will never see that terrible time.

Where will you be? Again the answer is clear. You will be with the Lord. Now the Bible indicates that two events will take place among the believers in heaven after the Rapture and before we come with Christ at the end of this period to reign with Him. a. The Bema Seat Judgment of Christ will take place when we shall be rewarded for the things done in the flesh. If you are a saved person, *you will be there.* Knowing that ought to make a difference in the life we live today!

b. Then the Marriage Supper of the Lamb will take place—the blessed moment when the bride (that is, you and I!) has made herself ready, dressed in her white robes of personal righteousness, and we are joined forever with the Lover of our souls, the Lord Jesus Christ. The Bible pronounces a blessing even on *guests* at that wedding. What must be the ecstasy of the bride!

2. **For the unsaved person.** If you have died before the Rapture, you simply will remain dead, in the torment of Hades.

If you are still living when Christ comes for His own, you will be left behind to endure those terrible events which the Bible calls the Great Tribulation. The Book of Revelation offers a vivid description of what you may expect: war, famine, pestilence, persecution, unnatural portents in the skies, supernatural plagues which will decimate the population of the earth, storm, fire, hail, demonic visitations, painful stings from unearthly scorpions, poisoned drinking water, other torments so dreadful that men will crawl into the caves and holes of the earth and cry for the stones to fall on them, until men who never pray will pray for death and cannot die. You will experience the terrible dictatorship of that Satan-inspired superman who will make you an abject slave to his will.

If you die during this period, you will go to Hades and join those unsaved ones who have died before you, there to await your final judgment.

If you live through this period, you will be killed at the great battle of Armageddon, at the spoken word of that Lord whose offer of salvation you have been spurning during this age of grace. Or you will stand before His judgment throne when He sets up His kingdom and hear Him say, "Depart from me, ye cursed, into everlasting fire, prepared for the devil and his angels" (Matt. 25:41).

In any case, you will die. *Not a single unsaved person will live* to enter the glorious kingdom of peace and prosperity and blessedness foretold by the prophets.

IV. During the Kingdom Age

For a thousand years Christ will reign on this earth on the throne of David. It will be a glorious time, when God will demonstrate what a wonderful world this world can be when it is run right. We continue to trace the destinies of the saved and unsaved.

1. **For the saved person.** You who are now saved will be in that kingdom. When Christ comes in power and glory to reign over the earth, all his saints will be with Him. "And the armies which were in heaven followed him upon white horses, clothed in fine linen, white and clean" (Rev. 19:14; cf. v. 8). "They lived and reigned with Christ a thousand years" (Rev. 20:4, 6). Jesus had told His disciples: "I go to prepare a place for you. And if I go and prepare a place for you, I will come again, and receive you unto myself; that *where I am, there ye may be also*" (John 14:2-3). To His apostles He said, "Ye . . . shall sit upon twelve thrones, judging the twelve tribes of Israel" (Matt. 19:28). In His parable the nobleman, when

he returned after receiving his kingdom, rewarded his faithful servants by giving them authority over ten cities and over five cities (Luke 19:17, 19). We don't know, of course, just how it is going to work out, or what the method of organization will be in that kingdom, but it is absolutely clear that you and I, who are part of His saved ones today, will reign with Him then. His church, the bride, will sit beside Him on His throne! In our glorified resurrection bodies we shall be associated with Him in the government of that era.

2. **For the unsaved person.** You who are not saved will have no part in the glorious kingdom of which we have been studying. You will have died before that kingdom begins. And you will remain dead, your body in the grave and your soul in torment in Hades.

V. At the Great White Throne Judgment

At the end of the kingdom age and the beginning of the eternal state one more great event will transpire according to prophecy, the judgment of the dead at the Great White Throne. What will this mean?

1. **For the saved person.** The saved person will not be present at the Great White Throne. When a sinner accepts Christ and becomes a Christian, he passes from death unto life. His sins have been judged at the cross of Christ, and he will never again come into judgment for his sins. "There is therefore now no condemnation to them which are in Christ Jesus" (Rom. 8:1). We shall stand before the judgment seat of Christ to be rewarded according to our works, but that takes place in heaven after our catching up to be with the Lord. This judgment at the Great White Throne is the judgment of "the dead," and the saved are no longer dead; they have been alive again for a thousand years. This judgment has nothing to do with the saved person.

2. **For the unsaved person.** All down through the ages of human history men have been dying. And death will continue to claim men until the end of the thousand-year reign of Christ, when the last enemy, death, will have been brought into subjection to Christ. When a man dies, his body returns to the dust from whence it came. The spirit or soul goes to the place God has prepared for such, to await God's judgment. "It is appointed unto men once to die, but after this the judgment" (Heb. 9:27). Before the kingdom

age begins, God takes out from among the dead all the saved folks in the first resurrection. So the only ones left in death are the unsaved. By the time the Millennium is passed, *all* unsaved are dead; the last to die are those rebels whom Satan gathers out at the end of the kingdom age (Rev. 20:7-9). From this point on there will be no more sinners, so the time has come for God to deal with all the unsaved of all human history in one great judgment day, the Great White Throne.

If you are an unsaved person, you will be there. God will raise you back to life in order to stand there. Your soul will come from Hades to re-possess your body now brought back to life, and as a whole man you will face your Judge. That Judge will be the Lord Jesus Christ, who has been seeking to get you to accept salvation now, whom you have been refusing. As you stand before Him, the books which have recorded your life will be opened before you. You will see written therein every deed you have ever done, every word you have spoken, every thought you have cherished, every motive you thought would be hidden. Those books will record every time you heard the gospel invitation and passed it by. Your mouth will be stopped. There will be no denial, no rebuttal, no excuses, nothing to say. Should you say, "Lord, Lord, have we not prophesied in Thy name and in Thy name done many wonderful works?" the Judge will turn to the book of life and search in vain for an entry which says, "So-and-so received Christ and has been given everlasting life." Then He will turn to you and say, "I never knew you: depart from me, ye that work iniquity" (Matt. 7:21-23).

You will watch as the angels add up the sum of all the evil things that you have ever done, and figure out the measure of penalty which you will be called upon to endure throughout an eternity in hell. Then, you will be cast into the lake of fire.

VI. Throughout Eternity

1. **For the saved person.** This will be "heaven," all that is involved in the eternity of blessedness for the redeemed. John struggles to describe it in those mysterious last chapters of the Book of Revelation. He speaks of a new heaven and a new earth, the universe renovated and forever done with the curse of sin; a new Jerusalem in which God will tabernacle with His people. There will be no more tears, no more death, nor sorrow, nor

crying, no more pain, free access to the fountain of the water of life. He describes the walls of the city, the gates of pearl, the streets of gold. The crowning glory of it is the Lamb himself, filling it with the light of His presence.

I am sure our present powers of comprehension are not adequate to appreciate all these revelations of His preparation for us. But we will have a whole eternity of unending opportunity to enjoy it and to worship Him who made it possible by redeeming us by His own precious blood.

2. **For the unsaved person.** You, too, are mentioned in connection with this glorious picture. But your place is not *in* the picture, rather on the *outside.* *"Without* are dogs, and sorcerers, and whoremongers, and murderers, and idolaters, and whosoever loveth and maketh a lie" (Rev. 22:15; read also 21:8, 27). You will be in the lake of fire. For you it will mean a second death, as that fire does its terrible work of destroying both body and soul in an unending torment.

SUMMARY

God divides men into two distinct groups.

The point of division is the cross of Calvary.

Your response to the message of salvation determines which path you will follow through the events of the future.

You can still decide which fortune you want for your own.

12

Signs of the Times

INTRODUCTION

The expression "signs of the times" has its origin in the words of our Lord when He answered the unbelieving Pharisees and Sadducees of His day who were asking for a sign, or a proof, from heaven as to His identity and authority. Jesus said, "Ye can discern the face of the sky; but can ye not discern the signs of the times?" In other words, there were plenty of signs, or proofs, showing around them. But they didn't use the same sense with regard to the Messiahship of Jesus that they did with regard to the weather indications.

The Bible indicates that there will be signs, advance indications, which will point to the approaching events of prophecy. Jesus himself said, "When ye see these things come to pass, know ye that the kingdom of God is nigh at hand" (Luke 21:31). Paul, in writing about the coming of the Lord, warned that His coming would be "as a thief in the night"; but he went on, "Ye, brethren, are not in darkness, that that day should overtake *you* as a thief. Ye are all . . . children of the day" (I Thess. 5:4-5). As signs multiply all around us, we have no excuse for not being prepared and ready. So it is a duty to be aware of the "signs of the times."

THE AIM

We want, then, to learn just what are the advance indications which will mark the near approach of the events of prophecy, the end of this age, and the second coming of Christ. We will want to see what influence these signs should have on our lives.

THE DEVELOPMENT

There are many passages of Scripture sometimes interpreted as signs which probably are wrongly used, and some which perhaps rightly are used as signs, but which we shall not attempt to include in our present study. The signs which we want to deal with may be classified under three headings.

THE EXPOSITION

I. Signs in the World

Our Lord himself pointed our attention to the conditions and events of the world as a sign of His coming.

1. **The sign of a despairing world** (Matt. 24:3-8; Luke 21:25-26). When the disciples came to Jesus asking specifically regarding signs of His coming and of the end of the age, Jesus pointed out to them the conditions that would prevail in the nations of the world. He spoke of "wars and rumours of wars"; He declared that "nation shall rise against nation, and kingdom against kingdom: and there shall be famines, and pestilences, and earthquakes, in divers places." Note carefully, however, that Jesus did not limit these to the time of the end. In fact He said, "All these things must come to pass, but the end is not yet. ... All these are the beginning of sorrows" (Matt. 24:6, 8). It would seem that these signs would characterize the entire age of the end times, and the fact that they are called "the *beginning* of sorrows" suggests that they may keep getting worse as the end comes closer. This seems to be the special point as Luke records it: "There shall be signs in the sun, and in the moon, and in the stars; and upon the earth distress of nations, with perplexity; the sea and the waves roaring; men's hearts failing them for fear, and for looking after those things which are coming on the earth" (Luke 21:25-26). The reference to signs in the heavenly bodies makes this apply to the very end of the age, immediately before the actual coming of the Lord, as also do the words of verse 27. Therefore, the sign of the distressed nations is a sign of the very end of the end time.

Is this sign manifest in the world today? As Jesus taught, there have been wars and rumors of wars all through this age. We certainly have them today! And I believe that any observer will agree that this distress of nations has been getting worse and worse, until today the whole world of men are on the brink of despair. H. G. Wells, the eminent historian, long before this last series of world conflicts were touched off by World War II, made the statement: "Destruction is not threatening civilization, it is happening to civilization before our very eyes. The ship of civilization is not going to sink in five years, nor in fifty years. *It is sinking now.*" It used to be said that every generation must have its war. But the present generation has seen two major world wars and a never-ending series of smaller wars, both hot and cold. The younger generation right now has never seen a day of peace! The desperation of the world today is a sign that the end of the age is drawing near.

2. **The sign of a depraved world** (Luke 17:26-30). Another sign Jesus gave to describe the conditons in the world at His coming was a comparison with the days of Noah. "As it was in the days of Noe, so shall it be also in the days of the Son of man." He went on to characterize those times: "They did eat, they drank, they married wives, they were given in marriage. ... they bought, they sold, they planted, they builded ... until the day that Noe entered into the ark, and the flood came and destroyed them all." Comparing this brief summary with the account in Genesis 6 of the days before the Flood, we get a picture of the conditions to which Jesus was referring, a picture of such depravity that God had to destroy most of mankind from off the earth. It is a picture of broken lines of separation, moral collapse, preoccupation with sex, particularly in its abnormal forms, violence, materialism, and secularism. All were "doing what comes naturally" right up until the day the Flood came—blind to all warning and deaf to the preaching of Enoch and Noah.

Again the description is such an apt way of characterizing conditions in our own day. Worldliness mingled with the church until it is impossible to tell a child of God from the children of the devil, moral degeneracy, crime, violence, passion, the perversion of sex into a national false religion with its idols and heroes and unspeakably hideous rites of worship, and over and through all the preoccupation with the affairs of everyday business which makes men blind to and wholly unconscious of all spiritual realities—these describe all too well the conditions of the world today. A depraved world is a sign of the approaching second destruction of the world at the coming of Christ.

3. **The sign of a developing world.** As we attempted to show in an earlier chapter, prophecy has much to say about the course of events in the nations of the world at the time of the coming of Christ and the setting up of the messianic kingdom. If we can see these events beginning to shape up in the world around us, these become signs which indicate that the time of their fulfillment may be drawing near. And it is the conviction of many students of Bible prophecy that our present world is developing into the situation which prophecy indicates it will be in when Jesus comes.

The revival of Rome is one of these signs. Prophecy foresees in the end time a Gentile world power which will in some sense be a continuation of the old Roman Empire, but in a form represented by ten kings, or a ten-kingdom confederacy. This, of course, has not yet come to pass, but there are some interesting developments. It is frequently noted that the present division between the eastern and western powers in Europe roughly corresponds to the ancient boundary of Rome, even to the detail of a divided Germany. Also, the European Common Market seems to be a possible beginning to a confederacy of many kingdoms which formerly were a part of Rome. This current economic interdependence could well form a basis for further political and social unity.

The prominence of Russia may be a development foreseen in prophecy as the northern power which invades Palestine and opposes the Antichrist in his rise to world domination. Certainly Russian communism is *not* the Antichrist, and will not be the final form of world power, although if the Lord delays His coming we have no way of knowing how far this northern bear may be allowed to go before he meets his doom at the hands of God in the mountains and valleys of Palestine.

Perhaps even more significant is the way the world is being prepared for a world government and for a dictatorship. Totalitarianism is on the rise all over the world, even in so-called democratic America, where our precious personal freedoms are being eaten away by the growing power of a central welfare state. Most of the world today is being ruled by dictators. And the cry everywhere is for a unified world government. The United Nations and its associated organizations are rapidly getting the world accustomed to thinking in terms of one world. All this is but preparing the way for the rise of Antichrist and his superstate in the end time.

II. Signs in Israel

In a previous chapter we dealt with the nation of Israel in prophecy. There we indicated that sometime before the awful judgment of the day of the Lord and the time of Jacob's trouble there must be a partial return of the Jews to their land of Palestine, and some measure of national autonomy there, in order that the prophesied covenant with the Roman prince may be made. Also the suffering of those days falls on the nation of Israel in Palestine and Jerusalem, as well as in their dispersion. So the return of part of the Jews to Palestine and the setting up of the sovereign state of Israel in our days has become one of the most convincing of all signs that we are nearing the end of the age.

Now, for the first time in over eighteen hundred years, the Jews are nationally and geographically where prophecy pictures them to be in the end time! Already over fifty Jews have gone back to Palestine for every one that returned from the Babylonian Captivity. Remarkable feats of scientific, technological, agricultural, and sociological transformation have taken place in the land. The nation vibrates with the enthusiasm of the frontier, and national pride is high. They are taking a prominent place in the council halls of the nations of the world, highly respected by almost all except their Arab neighbors. They are still in unbelief; they still violently reject the claim of Jesus to be their Messiah. In fact, the modern nation of Israel for the most part is nonreligious. A small minority is preserving the traditions of Judaism, but the vast majority has little use for even its Jewish religious heritage. Modern Zionism is not a religious movement. It is political and sociological. They show great interest in the Bible, even the New Testament, but to them it is a history book of their nation's past, not a divine voice calling them to repentance and faith. Even this unbelief is a sign, for that is exactly the picture of Israel portrayed by the prophets when the judgments of the end time are to fall.

III. Signs in the Church

Some of these have already been discussed, but we will gather together here some of the specific indications of the near approach of the end.

1. **False teachers** (I Tim. 4:1; II Tim. 3:6-8). The Bible leads us to

expect that as this age draws near its close there will be many false teachers, departing from the faith, giving heed to seducing spirits and doctrines of devils, men who resist the truth, men of corrupt minds, reprobate concerning the faith. Even in Paul's day Satan had his men who transformed themselves into the apostles of Christ as ministers of righteousness. So we may expect that in the closing days of this age these satanic ministers will infiltrate more and more the ranks of the ministry in the churches. Today, the *majority* of the pastors and ministers of the churches do not believe the Bible and its basic teachings, and are teaching a false gospel of righteousness instead of the grace of God and salvation by the blood of Jesus Christ, God's Son.

2. **Apostasy** (II Thess. 2:3). Closely related is this sign of a growing apostasy. Not only will there be false teachers leading men away, but there will actually be on the part of ministry and laity alike, a turning aside from the true Gospel. The word "apostasy" refers to a turning away from, a renouncing of, a faith formerly professed. Today false teachers are not coming from outside the ranks of Christendom, but from *within* it. And the vast majority of those who profess to be Christians in the world today are apostate. They have renounced the faith once for all delivered to the saints in the Bible. Liberalism, modernism, neo-orthodoxy, are apostate religious movements. Even the "new evangelicals" are showing a tendency to bow to the apostates in their rejection of the full inerrancy of the Scriptures. This is the Spirit of our age; it's in the air. And it is a powerful sign of the end of the age.

3. **Scoffers** (II Peter 3:3-4). Ridicule and scoffing have always been some of Satan's most powerful weapons in attacking God's people and God's Word, and he is using it overtime in our day, as any Christian student knows who seeks to stand up for his faith in Christ and the Bible in the classroom. But in the last days Peter says that the doctrine of the second coming of Christ will especially be the object of this scoffing. "Knowing this first, that there shall come in the last days scoffers . . . saying, Where is the promise of his coming?" (vv. 3-4).

There is no doctrine of the Scriptures which is more ridiculed than this doctrine of the second coming of Christ and related prophetic events. Satan hates and fights the doctrine of salvation through the blood of Christ, and seeks to substitute his own false gospels. But he just laughs at this doctrine. When we mention our faith in Christ's personal return, even professed Christians characteristically express their scorn and pity at our "stupidity" by pointing to their forehead with a circular motion, so much as to say, "You are crazy"!

4. **The ecumenical movement** (Rev. 17:1). Probably no movement in modern church life has created the interest and caught the fancy of so much of Christendom as the move toward church unity, the so-called ecumenical movement. Protestant denominations are forsaking the precious doctrines which their founders loved and contended for so earnestly, in a passionate scramble to "unite" with anyone who has been bitten by the same bug. Even the precious principles of the Protestant Reformation are tossed aside as ecumenical leaders make overtures of surrender to Romanism, and the "home to Rome" march appears to be beginning.

Now, this is exactly what prophecy indicates will ultimately take place. In Revelation 17 John describes a figure which seems to represent false religion in the end time. The existence of this figure presupposes a movement which will ultimately bring about a great union of all apostate religions. Of course, this ecumenical church of the end time may not become a reality until after the removal of the true church in the Rapture. But its beginnings today may well be a sign of the approach of that day.

5. **The Laodicean period** (Rev. 3:14-22). We have already studied this passage of Scripture and will mention it here only to show its significance as a sign of the end time. If Revelation 2 and 3 give us a prophetic outline of the periods of the church in this age, and if we are now living in the last of these periods, then the end of the age of the church is drawing near. The lukewarmness and spiritual indifference which characterized the Laodicean church and which characterizes our present period are a strong sign of the approaching end of the age.

SUMMARY

There are many signs foretold in Scripture and now being fulfilled around us which point to the near end of this age and the soon coming of Christ.

All these signs, particularly those in the world and in Israel, are signs of the second coming of Christ in power and glory, *not* signs of the Rapture.

Therefore, the coming of Christ into the air to catch away His people is even nearer than the signs would indicate, for the Rapture will precede the Revelation by seven years.

All of these signs, especially those in the church, are already being seen. They are already fulfilled in such measure that the end of the age could be upon us at any moment. Of course, if the Lord delays His coming we may expect these signs to intensify until He comes. But they don't need to intensify; they are already true.

There is not a single prophecy in the whole Word of God which must be fulfilled before the Lord comes.

"And when these things begin to come to pass, then look up, and lift up your heads; for your redemption draweth nigh" (Luke 21:28).

13

Prophetic Teaching:
Its Practical Values

SUGGESTED BACKGROUND DEVOTIONAL READING

Monday—Citizens of Heaven (Phil. 3:17—4:5)
Tuesday—When Christ Shall Appear (Col. 3:1-7)
Wednesday—Looking for That Blessed Hope (Titus 2:7-15)
Thursday—What Manner of Persons (II Peter 3:11-18)
Friday—When He Shall Appear (I John 3:1-9)
Saturday—Occupy Till I Come (Luke 19:11-27)
Sunday—Ye Shall Be Witnesses (Acts 1:6-11)

INTRODUCTION

Prophecy is a very practical doctrine. We began this book by insisting that our study of prophecy should not be merely for the sake of satisfying curiosity. We shall finish this course of study by pointing out the effects which it should produce in our everyday Christian living.

THE AIM

We have tried to direct each chapter to some specific purpose. Often these have been practical applications of the particular prophetic theme under consideration. Now our aim is to see that the Bible itself uses prophetic truth as a strong motivation for our Christian life and service.

THE DEVELOPMENT

There are so many and so varied exhortations in the Bible based on prophetic themes that we cannot touch them all. There seem to be three areas where the blessed hope of the coming of Christ will affect us.

THE EXPOSITION

I. Jesus Is Coming: Therefore, Be Holy

The teachings of prophecy are set forth in the Scriptures as a motivation for holy living, for living the kind of lives before God that are clean, pure, pleasing to God, and honoring to the name of Christ which we bear. There is no area of Biblical teaching more neglected than this in the evangelical churches today, as the low level of spirituality abundantly attests. For the Bible spends more time with teachings in the realm of Christian living than it does with any other teaching. For example, a sober and careful estimate based on actual count indicates that the Apostle Paul devotes ten verses to Christian living for every one verse on the doctrine of salvation. Now, what we are saying here is that prophetic truth will provide the motivation for holy living. We see it so often in the New Testament. Let's look at a few passages.

1. **Philippians 3:17–4:5**. The key verse here is verse 20. "For our conversation [citizenship] is in heaven, from whence also we look for the Saviour, the Lord Jesus Christ." Heaven is the country we belong to, and we are looking for the soon coming from there of our Lord. The verse begins with "for," and it is followed by "therefore" (4:1), so Paul is thinking of the practical effect of this doctrine.

Looking at the verses which precede, Paul has been describing the way *some* walk; earthly, fleshly, sinful. In contrast he has pointed them to his own example, and gives as the motivation for his own life and those that follow him, these prophetic truths of verse 20. "For . . . ."

Looking at the verses which follow, Paul draws a conclusion from the wonderful prospect which these prophetic truths hold forth: "Therefore . . ." (4:1). There follow some practical suggestions as to how we ought to walk in the light of Christ's coming and our heavenly citizenship: stand fast (v. 1); stop quibbling, get along with one another (v. 2); be helpful, cooperate in the work of the Lord (v. 3); be joyful (v. 4); be known among men for your "sweet reasonableness," the basic meaning of the word translated "moderation"; or, in other words, be pleasant and agreeable, easy to get along with (v. 5).

Note how he repeats the basic motivation at the end of verse 5: "The Lord is at hand." The realization of this prophetic truth will make a difference.

2. **Colossians 3:1-5**. Paul everywhere makes the doctrine of our union with Christ in His death, burial, and resurrection the basis of his doctrine

of Christian living. Here again he calls attention to it, and couples it with the blessed hope of Christ's return: "When Christ, who is our life, shall appear, then shall ye also appear with him in glory" (v. 4). He goes right on with the practical application. "Mortify therefore your members which are on the earth" (v. 5). The practical result of the realization that Christ is coming will be a progressive reckoning of ourselves dead to the world and the flesh.

3. **Titus 2:11-15**. Here is one of the most precious words of the Bible, "grace" (v. 11). It brings to mind all that our blessed Lord has done for us in His marvelous plan of salvation. Here Paul says that grace is a teacher, and what it teaches is holy living: "Teaching us that, denying ungodliness and worldly lusts, we should live soberly, righteously, and godly, in this present world." Then verse 13 bases this teaching of holy living squarely on prophetic truth: "Looking for that blessed hope, and the glorious appearing of the great God and our Saviour Jesus Christ."

4. **II Peter 3:10-14**. Peter here points us to two great themes of prophetic Scripture: (1) the certainty and awfulness of ultimate judgment on sin, and (2) the promise of a new order, in which righteousness dwells. Now note the forceful application he makes of these truths to *us*. Verse 11 says, "Seeing then that all these things shall be dissolved, what manner of persons ought ye to be in all holy conversation and godliness . . .?" Verse 14 says, "Wherefore, beloved, seeing that ye look for such things, be diligent that ye may be found of him in peace, without spot, and blameless."

5. **I John 3:1-5**. One of the most unbelievable doctrines of God's Word is the teaching that we shall be like Christ, found here and in many other passages. It is a likeness which begins at our conversion, grows throughout life, and is completed when we *see* Him at His second coming. Verse 3 gives John's practical application: "And every man that hath this hope in him purifieth himself, even as he is pure." This is the purifying hope. The hope of the coming of Christ and our glorious destiny to be realized then motivates us day by day to live pure lives as He is pure, to live more like Him *now* in view of our future likeness.

Notice, also, the verses which precede this precious promise. Note that I John 2:28-29 exhorts us to abide in Him, in view of His appearing, "that . . . we may have confidence, and not be ashamed before him at his coming." The knowledge that He is righteous (v. 29) and that we are going to stand before a righteous one tends to make us careful that we also be righteous, in order not to be made ashamed before Him when He comes.

> "Say nothing that you would not like to be saying
> When Jesus comes.
> Do nothing you would not want to be doing
> When Jesus comes.
> Go nowhere you would not want to be found
> When Jesus comes."

The next time you are tempted to sin, stop to remind yourself that Jesus may come at any moment, even while you are in the act of doing that forbidden thing. "Every man that hath this hope in him purifieth himself, even as he is pure."

II. Jesus Is Coming: Therefore, Be Busy

The second area in which the doctrine of prophecy produces a practical effect on us is in the matter of Christian service. We turn to Luke 19:11-13 for one of the clearest statements of this truth.

As Jesus drew near to Jerusalem on His last visit there, knowing that He would be rejected and crucified, and realizing that His disciples were still thinking of the immediate establishment of His messianic kingdom, He spoke a parable to them to make it very clear that the kingdom was to be postponed, and that a long period of time would elapse before He would return to set it up. "A certain nobleman went into a far country to receive for himself a kingdom, and to return" (v. 12). Obviously Christ is himself the nobleman. He is going into heaven, the far country. There He will receive His kingdom, to be handed over to Him by His Father as described in the Book of Revelation. Then, having received the kingdom, He will return to inaugurate that kingdom in the earth. This nobleman, before he went away, called together his servants and committed his affairs into their hands. His instructions were simple: "Occupy till I come." These are Christ's instructions to us His servants for the interval until He comes back. As such they are of special importance.

The word translated "occupy" is a business term. It means to busy one's self, to be engaged in business, to exert one's self, to carry on business, to make money by trading. In other words, Christ has turned His business over to us, to carry on His work until He comes again. His instructions are, "Be busy about My business until I come."

Perhaps we may summarize this responsibility under five tasks which our Lord has given us, all of them to be motivated by the knowledge of His coming.

1. **Be busy in missionary endeavor.** Jesus commissioned His servants with the task of preaching the Gospel to the whole world. His last words before He ascended were, "Ye shall be witnesses unto me both in Jerusalem, and in all Judaea, and in Samaria, and unto the uttermost part of the earth" (Acts 1:8). Then after He went up, while they were still standing there in wonder, two heavenly messengers gave them this motivation: "This same Jesus . . . shall so come in like manner as ye have seen him go into heaven" (v. 11). In Acts 15:14-17 God's purpose for this age is set forth. During this age He is calling out a people for His name. Then to encourage us in this task He promises, "After this I will return."

2. **Be busy in evangelism, in winning the lost to Christ.** One of the great chapters on soul-winning, II Corinthians 5, impresses on us the high privilege and responsibility of being ambassadors for Christ, urging men to be reconciled to God. In verse 10 Paul states as one of the motivating forces constraining us to this task the prophetic truth that "we must all appear before the judgment seat of Christ."

Paul found great encouragement and personal satisfaction in his work for Christ by contemplating the day when he would stand before Christ with those who had been saved under his ministry (I Thess. 2:19-20).

3. **Be busy in teaching the Word to the believers.** Soul-winning and missions represent only one of two functions which Christ commissioned the church to do. Not only are we to make disciples of all nations, but we are also to teach them to observe what Jesus taught. Here is a part of the business of Christ which is being terribly neglected in the church today, and with disasterous consequences. It has resulted in churches full of overgrown babies who have been won but not taught, born but not developed, well-nigh useless in the service of Christ. And the mortality rate of these "converts" is terrific. They go out the back door as fast as we bring

them in the front. We report so many converts every year, but our church isn't any larger or stronger than before.

It was to those who are faithfully carrying out both these tasks that Jesus gave the promise, "Lo, I am with you alway, even unto the end of the world [age]" (Matt. 28:20). This duty of teaching and caring for the people of God is the special privilege of the pastors. And to these under-shepherds a special honor and reward will be forthcoming "when the chief Shepherd shall appear" (I Peter 5:1-4).

4. **Be busy in doing good.** Good works are involved in the purpose for which God saves us, and the Bible encourages us to be rich in good works by pointing us to the prophecies of the future (I Tim. 6:17-19; cf. v. 14). After describing the resurrection and transformation which we shall experience at the Rapture, Paul concludes with the practical implication of this: "Therefore, my beloved brethren, be ye stedfast, unmoveable, always abounding in the work of the Lord, forasmuch as ye know that your labour is not in vain in the Lord" (I Cor. 15:58).

5. **Be busy in all the duties of the Christian.** The New Testament is filled with hundreds of exhortations, expressing our duties as the people of God. An amazingly large number of these are accompanied by a reminder of Christ's coming again as an incentive for doing them. We can do nothing more than to list some of these:

Love one another (I Thess. 3:12-13). Don't judge (I Cor. 4:3-5). Don't quarrel; get along with your brothers (I Cor. 6:1-2). Don't be engrossed in the cares of this life (Luke 21:34). Don't worry or be anxious (I Peter 1:13). Don't be ashamed of Christ (Luke 9:26). Be at peace (II Peter 3:14). Abide in Christ (I John 2:28). Keep the words of this Book (Rev. 22:7). Rejoice in trials (I Peter 1:6-7). Be patient (James 5:7-8). Let not your heart be troubled (John 14:1-3). Comfort one another (I Thess. 4:18). Be easy to get along with (Phil. 4:5). Be steadfast in sound doctrine (II Thess. 2:1, 15). Don't neglect going to church regularly (Heb. 10:25). All these exhortations are based on the second coming of Christ for their motivation.

III. Jesus Is Coming: Therefore Be Watching

A third area of practical application to the doctrines of prophecy has to do with our personal attitude of love and devotion to Christ himself. One of the commonest words on our Lord's lips as He spoke of His coming again was the word "watch" (read Luke 12:35-48; Mark 13:32-37; Titus 2:11-13; II Tim. 4:8). We should be watching for Him, looking for Him, longing for Him to come.

One interesting word used in the New Testament to describe this attitude is found in I Corinthians 1:7; Philippians 3:20; and other verses; translated "wait for" or "look for." The word combines in it not only the confidence that He is coming and the actual anticipation of His arrival, but it involves also a longing for Him. It says, we *want* Him to come, we are looking forward eagerly to His coming.

There are many reasons why we should look forward with eager anticipation to the coming of our Lord. a. His coming will mean the end of our troubles (Rom. 8:17-23), the end of our labor and toil and weariness. Now we get tired, worn out. All that will be over some day; Jesus is coming. It will mean the end of our sickness and pain. Some of us have been blessed with good health and we perhaps cannot appreciate this fully, but many of God's saints know what this means. It will be over soon; Jesus is coming. It will mean the end of our worry and anxiety. We know we shouldn't worry, but we do. Our faith is weak and our eyes are dim. We fret and are confused by the seeming prosperity of the wicked, but no more; Jesus is coming. It will mean the end of our sorrows, and separation, and grief. Every life has been touched with the sorrow of parting with loved ones. We know the heartache, the loneliness, even though "we sorrow not as others." But the time is coming when God will wipe away all tears; there will be no more death. We shall be caught up together; Jesus is coming.

b. We look forward to His coming because it will be our manifestation. Today we are laughed at, ridiculed, hated, despised. Satan and evil men are in control of world affairs. God's cause and God's people seem always on the losing side. But the time is coming when the true state of things will be made plain. God's plan and people will be manifested. Our cause will be vindicated; our true identity revealed. We look forward to that.

c. We eagerly anticipate Christ's coming because it will bring our reward. We all like pay days. We read with joy such passages as Revelation 22:12, Matthew 16:27, and I Corinthians 15:51-52 and 58, and reflect that all the labor and sacrifice will be repaid. It will be worth it all, when we see Jesus.

d. But the chief reason why we look forward with eager anticipation to the coming of Christ is Christ himself. *Jesus* is coming, our Beloved, the One we love. Our hearts swell up within at the prospect. We love Him, we long to be with Him. Above all else we want Him, we look for Him.

Peter expressed this sentiment in connection with the coming of the Lord Jesus Christ when he said, "Whom having not seen, ye love" (I Peter 1:8). Jesus' words of comfort to His troubled disciples reflect it: "Let not your heart be troubled. . . . I will come again, and receive you unto myself, that where I am, there ye may be also" (John 14:1-3). The glory of heaven will be the Lord himself: not the golden streets or the pearly gates, not the white robes or the crowns we have won, but Jesus Christ himself— to see Him, to hear Him, to be with Him.

SUMMARY

The doctrine of the second coming of Christ and other prophetic teachings are the most practical truths in all the Bible. They are the basis for almost every kind of practical exhortation.

They constrain us to holiness of life.

They inspire us to faithful service and the discharge of all our duties.

They stir our love and devotion to look for our precious Lord Jesus Christ.

These are reasons enough for studying this important theme of the Bible.